D1232691

Case Studies in Child and Adolescent Development for Teachers

Nancy DeFrates-Densch
Northern Illinois University

McGraw-Hill
Higher Education

Boston   Burr Ridge, IL   Dubuque, IA   New York   San Francisco   St. Louis
Bangkok   Bogotá   Caracas   Kuala Lumpur   Lisbon   London   Madrid   Mexico City
Milan   Montreal   New Delhi   Santiago   Seoul   Singapore   Sydney   Taipei   Toronto

McGraw-Hill
Higher Education

This book is printed on acid-free paper.

1 2 3 4 5 6 7 8 9 0 DOC/DOC 0 9 8 7

ISBN: 978-0-07-352585-3
MHID: 0-07-352585-5

Editor in Chief: *Emily Barrosse*
Publisher: *Beth Mejia*
Sponsoring Editor: *David S. Patterson*
Marketing Manager: *Sarah Martin*
Developmental Editor: *Emily Pecora*
Production Editor: *Holly Paulsen*
Manuscript Editor: *Mary Roybal*
Design Manager: *Andrei Pasternak*
Cover Designer: *Andrei Pasternak*
Production Supervisor: *Tandra Jorgensen*
Composition: *10/12 Times Roman by Aptara*
Printing: *45# New Era Matte, R. R. Donnelley & Sons*

Cover: SW Productions/Getty Images

Library of Congress Cataloging-in-Publication Data

DeFrates-Densch, Nancy.
  Case studies in child and adolescent development for teachers / Nancy DeFrates-Densch.
    p. cm.
  ISBN-13: 978-0-07-352585-3 (alk. paper)
  ISBN-10: 0-07-352585-5 (alk. paper)
  1. Behavioral assessment of children—Case studies.   2. Child development—Case studies.
  3. Classroom management—Case studies.   4. Classroom environment—Case studies.
  I. Title.
  LB1124.D44 2008
  305.231—dc22

                                                            2007021845

www.mhhe.com

To Andy, Alex, and all the other children and teachers who contributed their stories to this book.

Preface

It is important to understand children and adolescents in order to be effective as a Pre-K–12 teacher. Often students become so bogged down with the content of developmental course material that they "forget" about how the content is designed to bring developmental issues to life. This book is a collection of forty-one cases involving real children and their teachers. Each case is from two to four pages in length—long enough to give students the necessary information, yet short enough to be used in conjunction with other classroom instruction. The cases are based on fact; however, some creative license has been taken to disguise the identities of the parties involved.

✖ Benefits for Students and Instructors

- *To the students:* My sincere hope is that these cases will bring your textbook to life for you. Working with the material in context should help you better understand developmental theory and research. In addition, because these cases are based on fact, they offer a glimpse into the world of children and adolescents.
- *To the instructors:* This book is meant to be a companion to a development text. Each case can be used to help your students apply developmental theory and research to real-life scenarios. Cases can be used as either formative or summative assessment tools. They are also useful classroom discussion topics. I have used cases in my courses for years, generally breaking my class into small groups and assigning one case to each group. Following a group-work period, we come together for large group discussion of the cases. You can also use the cases as written assignments. Cases have been aligned with INTASC standards to facilitate course alignment.

✖ Key Features

- *Early Childhood Through Late Adolescence:* Cases range across the spectrum of developmental stages, from toddlers through high school, and include scenarios that reflect both typical and atypical development.
- *Comprehensive Range of Topics:* Scenarios tackle a wide range of issues that challenge today's teachers, including juvenile depression, the effects of divorce on children, parental neglect and abuse, and unhealthy/abusive romantic relationships.

- ***Questions for Reflection and Analysis:*** Suggested questions follow each case to guide student learning.
- ***Easy to Search:*** All cases are indexed according to age group, topic, and INTASC standard.

✖ Acknowledgements

I would like to thank the following individuals for their invaluable feedback in reviewing and commenting on this text in various stages of development:

Alan Bates, *Illinois State University*
Ioakim Boutakidis, *California State University, Fullerton*
Erika Burton, *Roosevelt University*
Judy Collmer, *Cedar Valley College*
Jeanne Galbraith, *Ohio State University*
Judith Geary, *University of Michigan–Dearborn*
Beverly Klecker, *Morehead State University*
Dennis Lichty, *Wayne State College*
Carol Marchel, *Winthrop University*
Sharon McNeely, *Northeastern Illinois University*
Lisa Pescara-Kovach, *University of Toledo*
Kathy Pillow-Price, *Arkansas State University–Beebe*
Dorothy Louise Justus Sluss, *Clemson University*

Case Matrix

Case	Page Number	INTASC Standards	Age Range				Topic															
			Early childhood	Middle/late childhood	Early adolescence	Late adolescence	Physical development	Cognitive development	Information processing	Motivation	Exceptionalities	Language/literacy	Self/identity	Gender	Moral development	Emotional development	Peers	Sexuality	Dating and romantic Relationships	Families	Culture	Classroom management
1. Potty Lottie	1	2,3,5,9	x				x	x								x						x
2. Recess	3	2,3,5,9		x			x			x				x		x	x					x
3. Please Don't Pick Me!	5	2,3,4,5,6,7,9			x		x	x		x			x	x		x	x					x
4. I Can't Go Back to School!	7	2,3,5,6,9			x		x	x					x	x		x	x					x
5. Socks	10	2,3,5,9			x		x	x					x	x		x	x					x
6. The Late Bloomer	12	2,3,5,9				x	x	x			x		x			x						
7. Body Image	15	2,3				x	x	x			x		x			x	x					
8. Plotting	17	1,2,3,5,6,9			x			x					x			x	x					x
9. Symbolism?	20	2,3,4,5,7,9				x		x														
10. Songs	22	2,3,4,5,7,9	x							x												
11. Chanting	24	2,3,4,5,7,9			x					x	x											
12. What on Earth?	27	2,3,4,5,7,9	x					x			x					x						x
13. Challenge	30	2,3,4,5,7,9			x		x	x			x											x
14. I Can Read!	33	2,3,4,5,7,9		x			x		x			x										
15. Mine!	36	2,3	x				x									x						
16. Tragedy	38	2,5,6,9			x		x									x	x					

Case	Page Number	INTASC Standards	Age Range				Topic														
			Early childhood	Middle/late childhood	Early adolescence	Late adolescence	Physical development	Cognitive development	Information processing	Motivation	Exceptionalities	Language/literacy	Self/identity	Gender	Moral development	Emotional development	Peers	Sexuality	Dating and romantic Relationships	Families	Culture	Classroom management
17. Depressed?	40	2,3,9				X										X						X
18. Who Am I Now?	43	2,6		X			x						X			X						X
19. Pants	46	2,3			X								X			X	x			x		
20. (Almost) All Grown Up, Now Where Do I Go?	48	2,3,9,10				X				x			X									
21. Dolls and Soldiers	50	2,3,5	X					x						X		X						X
22. Hallway Horseplay	52	2,3			X								X			X						X
23. Communication	54	2,3				X							X			X			X			
24. You're Gonna Get in Trouble!	56	2,3	X					x								X						X
25. I Told You!	58	2,3,5,6,9		X										X	X	X	X					X
26. Rules and Consequences	61	2,3,5,6,9,10			X			X		x			X		X							X
27. Morality or Health?	63	2,3,4,5,6				X		X								X		X			X	
28. Parental Involvement	66	2,5,9,10	X																	X		
29. Divorce	69	2,3,5,9,10		X				X		x						X					X	
30. The Target	72	2,3,5,9,10		X												X					X	X
31. Sit With Us—or Else	76	2			X			X						X		X	X					
32. Rejection	79	2,3			X									X		X	X					
33. The Boy	81	2			X									X					X		X	
34. What Did I Do?	84	2			X												X		X		X	
35. Because He Loves Me	88	2				X							X	X		X			X		X	

Case	Page Number	INTASC Standards	Age Range				Topic																
			Early childhood	Middle/late childhood	Early adolescence	Late adolescence	Physical development	Cognitive development	Information processing	Motivation	Exceptionalities	Language/literacy	Self/identity	Gender	Moral development	Emotional development	Peers	Sexuality	Dating and romantic Relationships	Families	Culture	Classroom management
36. Locker Room Bravado	91	2				X											X	X	X		X	
37. I Said No!	94	2				X								X				X	X		X	
38. She Wanted To	97	2				X								X				X	X		X	
39. Around the World	99	2,3,4,5,9		X				X		X												
40. Boys' School	101	2,3,4,5,6,9				X				X				X			X					X
41. The Only One	104	2,3		X													X				X	

Potty Lottie

Lottie is a very busy student in Ms. Pfeifer's kindergarten class. She enjoys most of the activities available in the class, from the doll corner to the blocks and trucks. Her favorite area is the science center, where she can touch all the things that Ms. Pfeifer has collected for the children. She particularly likes the collection of shells. Lottie is often so focused on the activity in which she is engaged that redirecting her attention is difficult. This is particularly true when Ms. Pfeifer tries to get her to join her classmates for a large-group activity.

One day Ms. Pfeifer brought in a new basket of shells for the science center. Lottie saw Ms. Pfeifer put the basket on the table in the science center before class began. She could hardly wait for center time so she could touch them. She had a difficult time focusing on the story Ms. Pfeifer read to the class because of her anticipation of playing with the new shells. As Ms. Pfeifer was finishing the story, Lottie began to notice that she needed to use the bathroom. However, just as she was about to ask, Ms. Pfeifer finished the story and announced, "Center time, children. Choose your center."

Lottie raced over to the science center and the new basket of shells before any other student could get there. Patty, who also liked shells, gave her a dirty look. Lottie began to sort the shells into piles by shape—flat shells in one pile, dish-shaped shells in another, spiral shells in still another.

As she picked up each shell, she said something about its shape, color, or size before placing it in the pile she decided it belonged. "Clam shell. Snail shell. Look at this one—I wonder what it is." None of the other children even looked at the shell Lottie was holding up in front of her. Lottie started a new pile with that shell and continued sorting.

As she was sorting, she fidgeted in her chair. "Lottie, do you need to use the bathroom?" asked Ms. Pfeifer.

Lottie looked around at Patty and at her piles of shells. "No, I'm OK, Ms. Pfeifer," she responded, thinking that if she left Patty would ruin her carefully constructed piles of shells and take the shells for herself.

She continued to fidget in her seat while sorting shells. Soon she was sitting on her foot, then with her legs crossed tightly. Suddenly, Lottie had a panicked look on her face. Then she began to cry.

"What's wrong, Lottie?" asked Ms. Pfeifer.

"I-I-I had an accident," Lottie answered quietly. There was a puddle of urine in Lottie's chair and on the floor around it. Lottie's pants were soaked.

"Oh Lottie, I asked you if you needed to use the bathroom, and you told me no. Now look at this mess," Ms. Pfeifer responded. "Now we'll have to call the janitor."

"Children, we need to go outside for some active play. Mr. Carson will need to work in here," Ms. Pfeifer said loudly to the class.

The rest of the class looked over at Ms. Pfeifer and Lottie. They started to snicker.

"Lottie wet her pants."

"What a baby."

"Potty Lottie, Potty Lottie."

"Children, stop that this instant," said Ms. Pfeifer. "Lottie had a little accident. That's all. Now go outside."

As the children filed out of the classroom, many of them were laughing about Lottie's accident.

"Let's get you cleaned up, Lottie. It's no big deal," Ms. Pfeifer comforted.

After school, when Lottie got on the bus, several of the other children began chanting "Potty Lottie, Potty Lottie." Lottie hung her head in shame.

Reflection Questions

- What are the issues in this case?
- What cognitive ability is Lottie demonstrating when she is sorting the shells?
- Considering the physical and cognitive development of kindergarten students, is Lottie's accident unexpected? Why or why not?
- What do you think of the way Ms. Pfeifer handled the situation? Why?
- What, if anything, would you do differently? Why?
- It is not unusual for "nicknames" such as Potty Lottie to stick with a child for a long period of time. How should Ms. Pfeifer handle it if the children persist in calling Lottie this name? Why?
- How might this incident impact Lottie socially?

Recess

Ms. Christensen teaches first grade at Proffer Elementary School. She has a very diverse group of twenty-five students. Several of her students have ADHD. Some have other mild disabilities. Some are gifted. One boy, Jacob, is gifted, has ADHD, and also has a learning disability. The group is ethnically and economically diverse as well. In spite of their differences, the children generally get along quite well.

Twice each day Ms. Christensen takes her class out for a 15-minute recess and monitors the recess herself. She observes them carefully in an effort to ensure their safety. For obvious reasons, hitting, shoving, and similar behavior are against the recess rules.

One Tuesday afternoon, Ms. Christensen observed five boys from her class laughing, shoving each other, and grabbing each other's shirts. "They know they shouldn't be doing that," she thought angrily. "I have had it with those boys! Why can't they behave more like the girls over there swinging?"

She walked over to where the boys were and said, "Jacob, John, Andy, Jamaal, Jason—stop this instant! That's it, you guys! No recess for you tomorrow!"

"Why?!" asked Jacob. "We're just goofin' around."

"You know it is against the rules to push and grab each other," replied Ms. Christensen.

"But we were just playing," retorted Jacob. "Nobody was getting hurt."

"Sorry, you know the rule. No recess tomorrow."

The boys appeared crestfallen. They were visibly upset that they would miss recess the next day. When they returned to the classroom, Ms. Christensen wrote all five of their names on the board as a disciplinary action. Jacob looked at the board and thought, "That's the seventeenth time my name has been on the board—more than anybody else."

On Wednesday morning, Ms. Christensen had the five boys sit along the wall of the building, at greater than arm's length apart, for the entire 15-minute recess. From there they watched the other children playing.

After morning recess, the children had language arts time. Jacob and Jamaal became very disruptive to the class. They were in and out of their seats. They talked out of turn. When it was their turn to read, they had no idea where to begin.

"Those boys are nothing but trouble," thought Ms. Christensen. "I guess maybe they should miss recess tomorrow, too."

Reflection Questions

- What are the issues in this case?
- How typical is the children's recess behavior? Tie your answer to theory and research regarding development and gender differences.
- What do you think of Ms. Christensen's practice of writing students' names on the board as a disciplinary action? Why? Tie your answer to what you know about children's cognitive and social-emotional development.
- What do you think of Ms. Christensen's taking away the boys' recess? Why? Tie your answer to what you know about children's physical and social-emotional development and gender differences.
- Do you think Ms. Christensen's interventions are likely to be effective? Why or why not? Tie your answer to developmental theory and research.
- Why do you think Jacob and Jamaal became disruptive? Tie your answer to what you know about developmental theory and research and individual differences.
- What would you do differently? Why? Tie your answer to theory and research.

Please Don't Pick Me!

Aaron is a 13-year-old student in Mrs. Rogers's eighth-grade algebra class at Madison Middle School. Like many of his male classmates, Aaron has recently experienced a growth spurt. He has grown 4 inches this school year alone. Growing so rapidly has caused him some problems in the wardrobe department, as well as some clumsiness. He has had to replace his pants three times to keep his ankles from showing. In addition to the obvious change in height, other changes have occurred. His voice has deepened, he has grown hair under his arms, and the hair on his legs has gone from light and downy to dark and coarse. He has developed pubic hair as well as the beginning of a moustache.

Aaron has also lost control of a portion of his anatomy. Without warning, he frequently becomes erect. This sometimes happens when he spots a pretty girl; at other times a fleeting thought is all it takes. Aaron finds this terribly embarrassing and is sure that he must be some kind of pervert. Surely, this doesn't happen to other guys. He certainly has never asked any of his friends about it! Talking to his parents is also out of the question—not because they would be reluctant to discuss pubertal changes, but because he wouldn't want them to think they were raising a pervert.

Mrs. Rogers has been teaching math at Madison for 15 years. She enjoys her job, finding young adolescents to be challenging but also interesting. She particularly enjoys teaching algebra. Her eighth-grade algebra students are those whose math achievement is well above average. They often excel in other areas of the curriculum as well. In general, they are well behaved, perhaps because she requires them to sign a behavioral agreement before she recommends their placement in algebra rather than pre-algebra.

Mrs. Rogers's class requirements include working problems at the board. She requires students to do this so she can engage in error analysis for both the student working the problem and the rest of the class. When she began this practice, she requested volunteers. However, she noticed that the same students—those who clearly understood the material—volunteered much of the time. This did not allow her to help students who were struggling. Now she randomly chooses students to work at the board. She has found this to be a good way to evaluate student understanding. She believes that if one student has problems with a particular concept, chances are another does as well. Because students don't want to appear unprepared when they are chosen to work at the board, they tend to pay attention. They like Mrs. Rogers and don't want her to be disappointed in them.

One warm spring day, Mrs. Rogers asks Michelle to work a problem on the board. Michelle is a very attractive girl. Her attire, while not risqué, shows off her mature figure, a fact of which she is well aware. Aaron is aware of it as well. He can't take his eyes off her while she works on the problem. As she is walking back to her seat, Michelle smiles at Aaron. He experiences a physical reaction—he develops an erection.

Mrs. Rogers scans the room, deciding whom to call on to work the next problem she has put on the board. As she looks around, Aaron silently begs, "Please don't pick me. Please don't pick me." But the unthinkable happens.

"Aaron, please go to the board and work on the next problem."

"I pass, Mrs. Rogers," answers Aaron.

"You can't pass, Aaron. Go work the problem."

"But Mrs. Rogers . . ."

"No buts about it, Aaron. Go."

Aaron silently ponders his situation. If he doesn't get up, Mrs. Rogers will probably give him a detention. He'll miss track practice, which means he won't be able to run at the next meet. He reluctantly gets out of his seat, pulling his shirt down as far as he can in an effort to cover himself. It doesn't work. As he passes Tyler, the class clown, Tyler says "Boner" in a voice just loud enough for students sitting close by to hear. They all start laughing. One student points at Aaron and says, "Hey, Woody." The laughter is contagious.

Aaron is mortified. He turns scarlet, grabs the nearest person's notebook, and runs out of the room to the sound of raucous laughter. Mrs. Rogers calls after him, but he doesn't stop.

Reflection Questions

- What are the issues in this case?
- Describe the perspectives of Aaron, Mrs. Rogers, and Tyler.
- How is this situation likely to impact Aaron's relationships with his peers? Why?
- Given what you know about early adolescent egocentrism, how is this situation likely to impact Aaron?
- Given what you know about early adolescent development, why do you think Aaron has not asked any of his friends if they experience a similar physical phenomenon?
- What do you think of Mrs. Rogers's edict that Aaron could not pass?
- How is this situation likely to impact the relationship between Mrs. Rogers and Aaron?
- What should Mrs. Rogers do now?

I Can't Go Back to School!

As Marcy and her friends enter Mr. Clark's eighth-grade English class, they are talking excitedly about the upcoming dance.

"Who are you going with, Marce?" asks Meagan.

"I don't know. I wish Brian would ask me," replies Marcy.

"Why don't you just ask him if you want to go so bad?"

"What if he says no?"

Just then Brian walks into the room.

"Shhh, Meagan. There he is," whispers Marcy.

Mr. Clark stands in the front of the room. He asks the students to take their seats and open their books to the chapter he assigned the day before. Most of the students quickly comply. Some take their time. Brian sits to the left and behind Meagan.

"I forgot my book, Mr. Clark," says David.

"I left mine in my locker. Can I go get it?" asks Mark.

"Boys, how many times have I told you that you *must* bring your books with you to class?"

"Hey, mine's at home because I was actually reading it. Mark's has been in his locker all semester," replies David.

"Mark, David, take a book from the shelf and use that. No highlighting. Take notes."

The boys go get their books, and the class gets down to business. The students break up into small groups to work on discussion questions that Mr. Clark has distributed. Marcy and Meagan are in the same group. Brian is in the group closest to them along with Mark and David. As Marcy's group works on a question regarding character analysis, a problem develops. Marcy raises her hand, and Mr. Clark comes by to see what she needs. "I don't think we have enough information to answer this question," she says.

"Marcy, why don't you go to the computer and check the Spark notes?"

"OK."

As Marcy gets up, Meagan notices a large red stain on her pants. She whispers loudly, "Marcy!"

"Huh?" Marcy says, as she turns around to see what Meagan wants.

"Sit down!"

"What?"

"Just sit down!"

"I have to go to the computer."

At this point, Mr. Clark notices that Marcy has begun her menstrual period. He has absolutely no idea what to do. He decides to allow Meagan to handle the situation, because she has already intervened.

"I'm telling you, Marcy, sit down before somebody notices," says Meagan.

"Notices what?"

Just then, Mark bursts out laughing.

"Too late, Marce," Meagan says. "I tried."

Marcy has a puzzled look on her face.

"Marcy. You've started your period," says Meagan.

"Oh, shit!"

Marcy can't seem to move for a second. Other kids begin to look at her. After what seems like at least 5 minutes to her but probably is closer to 2 seconds, she finally is able to move. She runs out of the classroom for the locker room as fast as she can. There she discovers that Meagan was correct. She has begun her menstrual period.

"Oh my God, I have got to get out of here!" Marcy changes into her PE clothes and goes to the office. Between sobs, she is able to explain to the secretary what happened. The secretary calls Marcy's mother and explains the situation. Marcy's mother takes an early lunch hour, picks Marcy up at school, and takes her home.

"Go change, and I'll take you back to school, honey."

"I can't, Mom!" Marcy cries.

"What do you mean, you can't? Just go wash up, put on some different clothes, pick up some supplies, and I'll take you back. I have to get back to the office."

"Mom, I can't go back to school. I just can't! Everybody saw! They all know. By the time I get back, the whole school will know!"

Reflection Questions

- What are the issues in this case?
- How unusual is it for a girl to begin her menstrual period and be unaware of it?

- Mr. Clark decided to allow Meagan to deal with the situation. Was this the right call? Why or why not?
- What would you have done differently if you had been in Mr. Clark's situation?
- What are some other possibilities?
- In what ways does the sex of the teacher impact the possible solutions? Why?
- Why does Marcy say that she can't return to school?
- How realistic is Marcy's statement that the whole school will know what happened to her by the time she gets back to school?
- How is this incident likely to impact Marcy socially?

Socks

It is the start of another exciting school year. It is always very warm at the beginning of the school year, and the building has no air conditioning. As a result, for the first month or so, the administration generally takes a looser approach to the dress code than normal. The concession made is that sleeveless tops are allowed, although thin straps are still disallowed. Most of the girls take advantage of the opportunity to wear tank tops.

As Mr. Green observes his sixth-grade class engaging in a hands-on activity, he takes stock of them. They are an interesting and diverse group. Most of the girls are taller and look older than most of the boys. In fact, while the girls look like young women, the boys still look like little boys. There are exceptions, of course. Zack is as tall as Mr. Green, is muscular, and even has a moustache. Jillian is petite and looks no older than Mr. Green's 9-year-old daughter.

This is the students' first year of middle school. Five elementary schools feed the middle school, and the students are mixed in their sixth-grade classes. As a result, while students probably know at least a few students in their classes, the majority of students are new faces. They are still getting to know one another. Mr. Green considers it part of his responsibility to ensure that the students form a cohesive team rather than segregating themselves based on elementary school. To this end, he assigns students to heterogeneous collaborative groups, making sure they work with students who did not attend elementary school with them. He monitors group work closely so that he can intervene if any problems arise.

As his students continue their group work, Mr. Green notices that Kristin has a sock sticking out of the arm of her top. "She must not have used fabric softener," he thinks.

Two boys in Kristin's group begin poking each other in the ribs and chuckling. They speak in low tones. "Get a load of that. She's stuffing herself!" James says.

"Damn! I knew she couldn't have grown that much over the summer," responds Jakob.

Kyle overhears the boys talking and joins in. "What should we do? Wanna pull it out?"

"I dare you, dude," says James.

"What'll you give me if I do?" asks Kyle.

"You yank the sock and I'll do your math homework for a week!" responds James.

"Guys, you can't do that," says Jakob.

"Watch me!" says Kyle.

He stands up and walks up behind Kristin. He grabs the sock. "Hey, Krissy, what's this?" he asks with a chuckle.

Kristin appears mortified and pulls away. Kyle pulls harder, removing the sock. Kristin's formerly voluptuous figure flattens immediately—well, half of it does. Kyle twirls the sock over his head while yelling "Whoooo-hoooo!"

Kristin leaves the room in tears.

Reflection Questions

- What are the issues in this case?
- Describe the situation from Mr. Green's perspective.
- Describe the situation from Kyle's perspective.
- Describe the situation from Kristin's perspective.
- How unusual do you think this situation is? Consider adolescent physical development and body image issues in your response.
- What could Mr. Green have done differently to prevent Kristin's humiliation?
- How should Mr. Green deal with the situation now?

The Late Bloomer

Josh is a 14-year-old Caucasian American of German descent. His father is 6 feet 5 inches tall and wears size 15 shoes. His older brother, who just graduated from high school, is 6 feet 2 inches tall and also wears size 15 shoes. His mother is 5 feet 6 inches tall.

Josh has always been extremely athletic and has played soccer and basketball since he was 5 years old. Because of his talent and his willingness to work hard to develop skills, he has always been the best player on the teams on which he has competed. If another player began to catch up to his skill level, he simply worked harder so he would remain the top player on the team. It was not unusual for him to practice several hours each day.

Josh has attended soccer camps every summer, often with his teammates. Coaches involved in the Olympic Development Program sometimes coached the camps he attended. These coaches spoke with Josh's parents and team coaches about Josh's talent and recruited him for their program. As he got older, he attended camps at area colleges and universities. The director of these camps generally was the coach of the college team. These coaches were equally impressed with Josh's skills, speed, creativity on the field, and work ethic.

One of Josh's dreams had always been to play soccer professionally. He often commented that he would be on the U.S. national team for the 2010 World Cup, when he would be 21. After this, he planned to play on a professional team in Europe. Of course, to accomplish this, he would first play soccer in high school, clubs, and college. He had chosen to attend a high school with a well-respected soccer program, relatively certain that he would receive a soccer scholarship to one of the top college soccer programs in the country.

During Josh's eighth-grade year, he noticed that other boys were growing at a more rapid rate than he was. Whereas when he was younger he was always among the tallest boys in his class, he was now one of the shorter boys, at 5 feet 7 inches. His best friend had had armpit hair since sixth grade. Josh had none. Some of the other boys had begun shaving their facial hair. Josh had no facial hair to shave—he still looked like a little boy facially. His jaw had not developed into that of a man. His feet and legs had begun to grow, however. In fact, most people would say that he was "all feet and legs." He wore size 13 shoes and had a 32-inch inseam. His shins were the same length as his father's. He was not as muscular as many other boys on his team, although he had begun to gain weight. As his feet and legs grew, his running style became awkward and his speed diminished markedly. While he had once been among the faster boys on his team, he was now the slowest. In addition, his stamina declined. He became winded much more easily than in the past. Of course, all these things negatively impacted his soccer game.

However, Josh still had aspirations of playing soccer professionally. Between eighth grade and his freshman year in high school, he participated in a summer soccer league with other boys who would be attending his high school. To his astonishment, he was not among the best players on the team. He was much slower than the others and sometimes tripped as he ran down the field. However, he still "had a nose for the goal" and had several shots on goal when he was in the game.

Josh also attended a residential camp at a nearby university in preparation for high-school tryouts. A man who had been the leading scorer on a World Cup Championship team coached this camp. At the camp Josh had some problems with dehydration, which caused severe cramping. After one bad night, however, he bought several bottles of sports drinks and kept himself better hydrated, alleviating the cramping problem. Although Josh was among the slowest players at the camp, the coach was very encouraging. He told Josh that he had great skills and a "world-class shot" and that if he worked on his speed he could play professionally one day.

Thirty aspiring players showed up on the first day of freshman/sophomore soccer try-outs. There were twenty-two spots on the team. The initial day of tryouts involved a running test. Participants had to run as far as they could in 11 minutes. While Josh was not the absolute slowest of those trying out, he was close. After the run, the players worked on skills and scrimmaged. During the skills drills, it was obvious that several of the players had never played soccer before. They had no idea how to trap or dribble the ball. Josh excelled in the drills and scored three times during the scrimmage. The high school coach told him that he had great ball-handling skills and a wonderful shot but that he would have to do better on the run to make the team.

Josh tried the run again the next day. While he went a little farther in the 11 minutes, he did not make it to the cutoff point. He participated in the scrimmage and scored again. The coach allowed him to try the run again after the scrimmage. Josh was tired and ran an even shorter distance than he had earlier. The next morning the three players who had not yet successfully completed the run met before practice to try again. Josh missed the cutoff by about a hundred yards. While he was discouraged, he tried again after the scrimmage. After 10 minutes, he was on pace to make the cutoff. However, during the last minute, he pulled a muscle in his leg and limped the rest of the way, failing to make the cutoff point. He did, however, finish the 11 minutes.

The coach and his assistant discussed their possible roster while the players scrimmaged. The assistant coach made a case for Josh's inclusion on the roster because of his advanced skills, indicating that as he developed he would regain his speed. The head coach stood firm on his position that Josh could not be on the team if he did not successfully complete the run. Several players who had poorly developed soccer skills but completed the run successfully were included on the roster.

After speaking with his assistant, the head coach decided to invite Josh to return the next morning to try the run again. Josh could barely walk, let alone run. He went home and iced his leg, hoping for a miracle. No miracle occurred. He called the coach and told him that he couldn't do the run because of his injury. The coach told him how sorry he was and again praised Josh's skills, but he was adamant that without successfully completing the run Josh would not be included on the roster. Josh was devastated. The coach invited him to be the team manager. Josh declined the invitation. It would simply be too painful to sit on the sidelines handing out towels and water bottles when he knew he should be out on the field.

Reflection Questions

- What are the issues in this case?
- Describe Josh's perspective of the events.
- Describe the high school coach's perspective of the events.
- What developmental factors contributed to Josh's not making the high school team?
- How do genetics contribute to Josh's developmental issues?
- How tall do you think Josh eventually will be? Why? Cite evidence from the case to back your position.
- What would you have done if you were the high school coach? Why?
- Do you believe Josh will try out for the soccer team next year? Why or why not?
- How do you anticipate not making the soccer team will impact Josh's high school experience? Why?

Body Image

Clarissa was a 16-year-old sophomore at Roosevelt High School. She was an average student academically. Clarissa was a pleasant girl who had one close friend, Jennifer, with whom she did just about everything. She had never had a boyfriend or even been on a date. When the other girls talked about dances and going to the movies with their boyfriends, Clarissa wondered if she would ever go out with a boy.

At 5 feet 6 inches tall, Clarissa weighed 250 pounds. Because of her size, she could not wear many of the fashions the other girls did. She had to buy her clothes in the "plus size" department of the local discount store, and the selection generally was not very fashionable. She wore loose pants and tops made of comfortable knit fabrics. Ever since Clarissa could remember, she had been the object of ridicule from her peers because of her size and her clothing.

"Hey, Clarissa!" shouted Robert, "Your class picture is gonna hafta be an aerial shot! You wear enough polyester to keep us dependent on foreign oil forever!" He and the boys surrounding him laughed uproariously.

Most of the time Clarissa tried to ignore the taunts of her classmates, but sometimes their comments hurt her deeply. Other times they made her very angry. Her mother, who was also large, tried to help Clarissa feel good about who she was and espoused the concept of "healthy at any weight."

"You don't understand, Mom," Clarissa protested. "I can't wear any of the clothes the other girls wear. I'm tired of this nasty polyester junk. I want to wear jeans. I want to wear what everybody else wears!"

"OK, Clarissa. We'll go to a specialty store. Maybe we can find some more fashionable clothes there. You won't be able to have as many though. The clothes will be much more expensive, and we just can't afford to do too much," responded Clarissa's mother.

"Thank you, Mom! I'll spend my baby-sitting money, too. One pair of jeans will be better than five pairs of those knit pants. Thank you so much!"

The next day after school, Clarissa and her mother went to a store for larger women. To Clarissa's delight, they found many clothes that were appropriate for girls her age. She bought two pairs of jeans that actually fit her and several tops that were similar to those worn by the smaller girls at school. Later she stopped by a cosmetics counter and learned how to apply makeup more artfully.

"I feel like a princess, Mom! Thank you for doing this!"

"You're welcome, Honey. You do look wonderful!"

For the first time in years, Clarissa was excited about going to school. She could hardly sleep the night before, thinking about walking into school with her new look. That morning, Clarissa carefully dressed in her new jeans and top. She took special care applying makeup the way the woman at the cosmetics counter had shown her. When she was finished, she felt wonderful about the way she looked. "This is it," she thought. "Nobody can make me feel rotten about myself today."

As she walked into school, her friend Jennifer spotted her. "Clarissa! You look awesome! I love the jeans! And wow! What did you do with your makeup? This is incredible!"

Clarissa beamed. "You really like it?" she asked.

"Uh, yeah! You look great!"

Clarissa's confidence soared. For the first time ever, she was noticed positively by some of her classmates. Several people commented on her new look—even a couple of the boys. "Lookin' good, Clarissa," commented John.

However, not all her classmates were impressed. Robert, as usual, was cruel. "Hey, look at Clarissa's new duds! What's your belt size, Tubby? Equator?" he laughed.

Clarissa gave him a scathing look. "I may be fat, but you're stupid, Robert, and I can always lose weight. You're stuck with your IQ!"

Robert was struck speechless as his friends laughed riotously. "Burn, dude! She got you that time!"

Clarissa smiled and walked away, holding her head high.

Reflection Questions

- What are the issues in this case?
- In recent years many schools have focused on fitness and nutrition in their PE and health courses. How do you think this focus might affect Clarissa?
- How could teachers have helped Clarissa?
- Why did Clarissa's confidence rise when she bought new clothing?
- In the end, Clarissa responded to Robert with a rude remark. Was this a good thing? Why or why not?
- How would you advise Clarissa to deal with the remarks of her peers?

Plotting

Liberty Elementary School is a small, rural K–8 school located in a very small town. There are approximately 250 students in the entire school, approximately 60 of whom are in grades 6–8. While there is little ethnic diversity among the students, there is a great deal of economic diversity. Some students receive free or reduced lunch from the state, while others are from extremely wealthy families. A great deal of diversity is also present in terms of parental education and occupation. Some parents did not finish high school; others have doctoral or law degrees. Parental occupations run the gamut from working at the local gas station to farming to teaching, practicing medicine and law, and engaging in business. The community even boasts a couple of retired professional athletes. For the most part, everyone in the community supports everyone else, and this support is reflected in the school.

During the first week of the school year, the middle-school students and their teachers take part in a team-building program offered at an outdoor recreation facility. The idea is for the students and staff to get to know one another and develop team spirit. This is a very popular activity, and students and faculty all look forward to it.

Ms. Xavier is in her third year teaching science at Liberty. She taught for several years elsewhere before taking time off to stay home with her own children until they were all in school themselves. She does not live in Liberty; her children attend school in the nearby town where they live. While Ms. Xavier enjoyed her first two years back teaching, this year she is having some problems. An influx of students new to the school appears to have changed the school's dynamics, making everything just a little bit more difficult—particularly discipline.

One new boy, Lucas, is particularly troublesome. While he is very bright, he is not nearly as compliant as the students to which Ms. Xavier has become accustomed. He is not always in his seat when the bell rings, and he often forgets his homework in his locker. Several times, Ms. Xavier has had to ask him to stop visiting with his friends and to get back to work. She finds this exasperating.

Lucas does not like Ms. Xavier at all. He thinks she has rules for the sake of having rules rather than for any particular purpose. He cannot understand why leaving homework in a locker is "such a big deal—at least I did it!" Ms. Xavier has problems with this kind of response. What she expects is an apology and an assurance that it won't happen again. Lucas simply will not comply.

One day during the unit on the solar system, Mark, another student in the class, asks, "Ms. X, why do the seasons change?"

Ms. Xavier responds, "Well, Mark, the seasons change because of the distance the earth is from the sun. You see, the earth travels in an elliptical pattern, and when we are farthest from the sun it is winter."

Lucas raises his hand.

"Lucas?" asks Ms. Xavier.

"I don't think that's right, Ms. X. The earth's orbit around the sun isn't very elliptical, it is nearly circular. The seasons have to do with how direct the suns rays on the earth are."

"Not true, Lucas," responds Ms. Xavier.

That night, Lucas checks on-line and finds that he was indeed correct. Just to double-check, he asks his father to explain it to him. His father's explanation matches the explanation given by the Web site.

The next day during lunch, Lucas, Mark, and Josh are talking. "I'm telling you, she's dumb," says Lucas.

"What do you mean?" asks Josh.

"That explanation she gave Mark about the seasons yesterday was wrong. She made it up."

"Are you serious?" asks Mark.

"Yeah, I looked it up last night," responds Lucas.

Lucas, Josh, and Mark all play on the school's basketball team. Their team will play Ms. Xavier's son's team Thursday after school. Ms. Xavier teases the boys about it in class during the week. "You guys just wait until the game Thursday night. My kid's team is going to whip your butts," she teases.

"You think so, huh? We're gonna dominate!" responds one of the boys.

"Well, I'll be there to see you guys get wiped off the floor."

Later the boys are talking with their teammates. "Can you believe she said that stuff?" asks Lucas. "She's cheering against us!"

As the boys arrive at the game, she reminds them that she'll be watching—and cheering for the other team.

Lucas finds her comments particularly upsetting. "Wow, that's supportive, Ms. X."

During the final quarter of a very rough and competitive game, one of the players from the other team actually tackles Lucas when he has the ball. Lucas goes down hard and stays down. The officials call for a jump ball. Fans from Liberty are angry. They believe a foul should be called, at the very least. Lucas has to be helped off the floor by his coach. After the game, he is nearly carried to the locker room by his teammates. He is limping badly when he emerges, and he complains of a sore shoulder during the ride home with his parents.

The next day, Lucas's mother takes him to the doctor. His shoulder has a minor separation, and he has a hip pointer. After the trip to the doctor, she takes him to school with a note for the coach saying that he can't play until he has been checked again by the doctor in a couple of weeks.

During science class, Ms. Xavier greets Lucas with "So, Mr. Injury, how are you doing today?"

"Well, aside from the separated shoulder and the hip pointer I got in last night's game, I'm OK. I spent the morning at the orthopedist's office—thank you very much."

Ms. Xavier is shocked. "I didn't know you were really hurt, Lucas."

"What did you think—I just wanted to sit on the bench for the rest of the game? I wanted Josh and Mark to carry me out? Geez!" Then, under his breath, "What a moron!"

Ms. Xavier moves on with her lesson.

During lunch, the boys talk about the game and about Ms. Xavier. "That was seriously rude, dude," says Josh. "I can't believe she dissed you like that 'Mr. Injury.' "

The more Lucas thinks about the incident, the angrier he becomes. The angrier he becomes, the more he wants to get even with Ms. Xavier. "Remember how she didn't know what causes the seasons, guys? Let's see what else she doesn't know. Let's all look stuff up. Then we can ask questions, and when she's wrong we can correct her and make her look like the idiot she is."

"Excellent!" replies Josh. "This is gonna be so cool!"

The boys carry out their plan. Each day one of them asks a question of Ms. Xavier. She never indicates that she does not know an answer. Instead, several times she gives incorrect answers. When she does this, one of the boys responds, "Well, not according to . . . ."

The other students in the class find this quite humorous. After several days of this treatment, Ms. Xavier realizes that the boys have conspired against her. She asks to speak to them and tells them not to do it anymore.

"Not do what, Ms. X? Ask questions?" responds Lucas. "We just want to learn," he says with a smile.

Reflection Questions

- What are the issues in this case?
- Describe the situation from Lucas's perspective.
- Describe the situation from Ms. Xavier's perspective.
- Based on information in the case, at which of Piaget's stages of cognitive development do you believe Lucas to be operating? Why?
- Why did Lucas set out to make Ms. Xavier look bad?
- How is this situation likely to affect Lucas's motivation in science? Why?
- What could Ms. Xavier have done differently to keep this from happening?
- What do you think of the team-building activities at the beginning of the school year? Why?

Symbolism?

Mr. Ramirez teaches English at Morgan High School. This year, his junior-level students are reading and analyzing several novels, among them *The Adventures of Huckleberry Finn,* by Mark Twain. Mr. Ramirez wants his students to really think about the novel and what it means. He expects his students to understand the themes and symbols contained in the novel, as well as the story.

Each week Mr. Ramirez assigns several chapters of the novel to be read. In class, the students discuss their understanding of what is happening in the book. The discussions focus on the facts of the book and on student predictions of what will happen next. Overall, Mr. Ramirez is happy with what the class is doing. For one thing, they appear to actually be reading the book, which is a step in the right direction. They also seem to remember much about the characters, setting, and plot. They engage in spirited debates about the characters and their actions.

Mr. Ramirez decides to break up the material in the novel for assessment purposes. He plans to give three quizzes and then a cumulative exam. He is surprised by some of the responses his students give to the exam items.

For example, on the exam, Mr. Ramirez asks, "Why does Twain use a child as the protagonist in this book?"

Barbara's response: "I have no idea what a protagonist is, let alone why Twain would use a child as one."

Jennifer's response: "It has to do with a comparison between the powerlessness of children and the powerlessness of black slaves during the time of the book."

Jake's response: "How on earth would I know why Twain did that? Ask him!"

Another question asks students to discuss Twain's use of the river as a symbol in the novel.

Barbara's response: "The river is just the river. It is the center of the boys' lives. They use it for navigation. They have fun around and on it."

Jennifer's response: "The river represents both freedom and change. It represents freedom in that it is wild. It represents change in that it is in a constant state of flux. A river is never stagnant, always changing, just like life."

Jake's response: "It is a river. The boys have adventures on it, so I guess it could mean something about fun."

Finally, Mr. Ramirez asks the students to tell the theme of the novel.

Barbara's response: "It is a book about boys having adventures on a river. They get into lots of trouble, but they always seem to escape."

Jennifer's response: "It is a book about the cruelty of slavery, about freedom and the changes that society was experiencing at that time."

Jake's response: "It's just a book about two guys who have a lot of fun and get into a lot of trouble."

"I can't believe these answers! It seems as if Jennifer is the only one who understood this book at all," he thinks. "What on earth can I do about this?"

He tries to explain the answers he was looking for on the exam but is met by many blank faces. In fact, only three or four students seem to have grasped the concepts contained in the book. Mr. Ramirez is frustrated and spends some class time explaining what symbolism is and how authors often use symbolism to get their points across.

Jake asks, "But Mr. Ramirez, how do we know Twain meant any of that junk? I mean, did he leave some sort of readers' guide to his books? I've always liked his stuff, but now I'm not so sure anymore. Reading shouldn't be this much work."

Barbara adds, "I'm with Jake on this one. Has anybody ever asked Twain about this, or is it just a bunch of stuff made up by English teachers?"

Later, Jake complains that he received a D on the test because he didn't "get any of that symbolism stuff." He grumbled, "His tests are impossible! Who thinks that stuff up?"

Reflection Questions

- What are the issues in this case?
- Explain the situation from Mr. Ramirez's perspective.
- Explain the situation from Jake's and Barbara's perspectives.
- At which of Piaget's stages of cognitive development do you believe each of the students discussed to be operating? Why?
- How do you feel about Barbara's and Jake's assertions that symbolism is "made up by English teachers" rather than incorporated into literature by authors?
- What, if anything, could Mr. Ramirez do to help future students understand *The Adventures of Huckleberry Finn* at the level he would prefer?
- Is the understanding of literary symbolism a reasonable expectation for juniors in high school? Why or why not?

Songs

Ms. Kalkman taught pre-kindergarten at Rockville Elementary School. Her students were a diverse lot—ethnically, economically, and with regard to prior knowledge. Ms. Kalkman wanted all her students to learn and believed that using music was a fun way to accomplish this. To this end, she taught her students a variety of songs. They generally began the school year by learning the alphabet song. She carefully explained that L, M, N, O, and P were separate letters, not one "elemenopee."

Soon after, they learned "Three Little Monkeys":

> Three little monkeys sitting in a tree, teasing Mr. Alligator, "Can't catch me."
> Along comes Mr. Alligator as quiet as can be, and SNAP!
> Two little monkeys sitting in a tree, teasing Mr. Alligator, "Can't catch me."
> Along comes Mr. Alligator as quiet as can be, and SNAP!
> One little monkey sitting in a tree, teasing Mr. Alligator, "Can't catch me."
> Along comes Mr. Alligator as quiet as can be, and SNAP!
> Away swims Mr. Alligator as full as can be.

In addition to the words, Ms. Kalkman taught her students gestures to go with different parts. For instance, when the monkeys tease the alligator, the children put their thumbs up by their ears and wiggled their fingers in a taunting gesture. Mr. Alligator's swimming was portrayed by placing one forearm on top of the other and moving both in synchrony. Finally, Mr. Alligator's snap was made by opening the arms and then clapping them together sharply. The children always laughed at the end of the song.

They also sang an old traditional favorite, "This Old Man," which involved much knee slapping:

> This old man, he played one.
> He played knick-knack on my thumb.
> With a knick-knack paddywhack, give your dog a bone.
> This old man came rolling home.

> This old man, he played two.
> He played knick-knack on my shoe.
> With a knick-knack paddywhack, give your dog a bone.
> This old man came rolling home.

It seemed that Ms. Kalkman had a song for everything. She taught her students "Head, Shoulders, Knees and Toes" in both English and Spanish. She taught them songs about the months of the year and the days of the week. By the end of the school year, her students had learned a United States of America song during which they sang all the names of the states in alphabetical order. Ms. Kalkman's colleagues often commented that hers was a musical classroom. People sometimes lingered in the hall just to hear her students singing.

The students performed their entire repertoire for their parents at their annual year-end concert. The parents weren't terribly surprised, because most of the children had been singing the songs at home for months. However, hearing them all together was impressive. The students and Ms. Kalkman received a standing ovation following the performance.

Reflection Questions

- Indicate the objective(s) of each song mentioned.
- Do you agree with Ms. Kalkman that music helps students learn? Why or why not? Tie your answer to information-processing theory and research.
- What purpose does the students' singing of the songs at home serve?
- Would the same learning have taken place if Ms. Kalkman had used more traditional teaching methods? Why or why not?

Chanting

M r. Alexander taught high-school Latin, which was considered an "honors class" because it was deemed more difficult than the other languages taught at the school, Spanish and French. Mr. Alexander was the oldest teacher at the school—far beyond the age at which most of his colleagues would retire. He was known to have high expectations and to be strict with his students. In spite of the difficulty of the subject matter and his strictness, Mr. Alexander's students genuinely liked him. He had become somewhat of a school icon and often was invited by the senior class to speak at graduation. This pleased him greatly.

Mr. Alexander's students frequently competed in Latin competitions, known as Certamen, and performed well. They also took both the state and national Latin exams. The majority of his students did quite well on these tests, finishing cum laude or higher. Mr. Alexander took great pride in his students' accomplishments, although he took no credit for them.

Mike was a freshman in Mr. Alexander's first-year Latin class. Early in the first quarter, Mike was struggling to keep his head above water in class. He decided that learning a new language, especially one like Latin, was more difficult than he thought it would be. It was all so confusing, especially conjugation—even nouns had to be conjugated in Latin.

"I just can't remember this stuff," commented Mike to a sophomore who had befriended him.

"Have you started chanting yet?" asked his friend, Joe.

"Huh?"

"Just wait. Once he starts the chants, you'll remember."

The next week, Mr. Alexander taught his students their first chant: "Bo bis bit bimus bitis bunt, Hey!"

At first the students responded tentatively and softly. "Louder!" Mr. Alexander commanded. The students chanted a little more loudly.

"Louder!" he again commanded. Soon the students were yelling the chant with enthusiasm.

"What on earth?" asked the new Spanish teacher, Ms. Martinez, as she and a colleague walked by the classroom.

"Oh, that's Mr. Alexander's class," responded Mr. Nedry, the other Spanish teacher. "His class is the loudest in the school. Always yelling."

"That doesn't sound like yelling. That sounds like some kind of chant."

"Whatever. It's annoying as heck when you're trying to get your students' attention."

Ms. Martinez decided she would listen more carefully to the noise emanating from Mr. Alexander's classroom. Each day his students repeated the same chant. They sounded very enthusiastic. Occasionally, Ms. Martinez heard Mr. Alexander command "Louder!" to which his students responded with even more enthusiasm. Ms. Martinez decided she would ask Mr. Alexander about the chanting.

"The chants? Oh, they're learning how to conjugate. See." He showed her a page from the Latin book that explained the meaning behind the chant.

-bo—future 1st person singular suffix
-bis—2nd person
-bit—3rd person
-bimus—future 1st person plural suffix
-bitis—2nd person
-bunt—3rd person

"And the kids learn it this way?" asked Ms. Martinez.

"Sure, it sticks in their heads. Here, let me show you something."

He showed her a letter he had received from a former student. The student thanked Mr. Alexander for his rigor in Latin and explained how it had helped him in his later studies in medicine. Rather than using a traditional closing to the letter, the student wrote, "Bo bis bit bimus bitis bunt, Hey!" followed by his name.

"I haven't seen this kid in over twenty years," explained Mr. Alexander, "and he still remembers. But don't tell anybody my secret," he said with a wink.

Ms. Martinez was astounded. After this, she decided to spend some time in Mr. Alexander's classroom. She spent several of her prep periods sitting in with his classes. She learned several other chants along with the students, including "us i o um o!" and, later in the year, "i orum is os is!"

Sometimes she overheard Mike and some other students chanting at each other during lunch or study hall. They even greeted each other in the hall with these chants.

That year Mr. Alexander's teams won every Certamen in which they competed. They finished second in the state tournament.

"Absolutely amazing," Ms. Martinez thought. "I'm going to have to figure out how to do this in Spanish."

Reflection Questions

- Why do Mr. Alexander's students like him so much, in spite of his age and strictness?
- Explain why the chanting works from an information processing perspective.
- Could this work in other languages? Why or why not?
- Could it work in other content areas? Why or why not?
- How could participating in competitions help students learn another language?

What on Earth?

Scottie was a student in Ms. Grant's kindergarten class. He was a very active, curious little boy. He was always busy with something—often not the things that Ms. Grant had asked the class to do. For instance, when the class was supposed to be coloring a picture so that it matched the model, Scottie chose different colors and even made his own "lines" within which to stay.

"Scottie, why aren't you coloring the picture like it is on the wall?" asked Ms. Grant.

"I don't like it that way. These colors look better together."

"But Scottie, grass isn't purple," responded Ms. Grant.

"I know, but it sure would be cool if it was," answered Scottie, "so I made mine purple. I wonder what color milk would be if we had purple grass?"

"What do you mean?"

"Well, cows eat green grass and we get white milk. If they ate purple grass, would milk be a different color?" Scottie replied.

"Whoa," thought Ms. Grant. "I really don't know, Scot. What do you think?"

"I think it would be blue," Scottie replied as he colored some clouds green.

Ms. Grant shook her head as she walked away. "I don't know about that kid sometimes," she said to herself.

A week later, Scottie was playing with small blocks with some other boys. Ms. Grant came over to see what they were doing. The boys had laid out several rows of blocks.

"I wonder if you can count these blocks for me," she challenged.

"There are seventy-two of them, Ms. Grant," responded Scottie.

"Did you already count them?" asked Ms. Grant.

"No. I don't have to," said Scottie.

"What do you mean you don't have to count them, Scottie?"

"Well, see there are eight rows of nine, so that means there are seventy-two."

Ms. Grant's jaw dropped open. She had never heard an answer like this from a 5-year-old. "Uh, very good, Scottie!" she said in amazement. She then made another array of blocks. "How many are there now, Scot?" she asked, thinking somebody had taught him the eight rows of nine "trick."

"Ms. Grant, there are only forty-eight now. Six rows of eight," responded Scottie with a grin.

Later that same afternoon, Scottie was playing with a puzzle of a United States map. As he put the pieces in the puzzle, he said the name of the state and its capital. Soon other children were watching him and handing him pieces. He placed each piece correctly, even if he did not yet have the adjacent piece, and again said the name of the state and its capital. Before long, Scottie had quite an audience. He began teaching and quizzing the other children. He held up each piece before he placed it, asking "What state is this?" Then he gave the correct answer. "And its capital?" he asked. This became part of the class routine during free time. By the end of the month, most of the students could complete the map, and many could name at least half the states.

Later in the school year, the class visited the school library to choose books. Most of the children chose picture books and beginning reader books. Not Scottie. He found a section of books about geography. There, among these books, he found a book all about flags from around the world. Scottie looked at the book with wonder. He got the book down and sat in the aisle looking at it. He turned the pages slowly, examining each flag and naming the country from which it came. When it was time to go back to class, he took his treasure to the checkout desk.

"Scottie, you can't check out this book," said Ms. Trolliet, the librarian. "You can only check out books from the blue section."

"Those books are dumb," responded Scottie. "I want this one."

"But Scottie, you can't read that book. It's for the older kids."

"I can so!" Scottie proceeded to name the countries of many of the flags to the librarian, who acquiesced and allowed him to check out the book.

Ms. Trolliet told Ms. Grant about the incident. "I know. He's very precocious," responded Ms. Grant. "Last week he took a novel off my desk and started reading it while I was working with another student. It was not an appropriate book for a kindergartner by a long shot!"

A group of boys was working together on the playground, trying to move the climbing rock. As they struggled, Scottie watched. Finally, he joined the effort. "Hey guys, we'll never move it like this. We need to get a long piece of wood and a smaller rock or something. If you get me those things, I think I can move this rock for you."

"Yeah, right, Scot!" said John.

"Hey, he can do lots of stuff. Let's get him that junk and see what he can do," said Jorge.

The boys found a fallen tree limb and a large rock. They brought them to Scottie. "See, we put the end of the limb under the rock and this other rock under the limb. Now we all need to push down on the other end of the limb and the rock will move," explained Scottie.

"Really!?"

"Yep. Let's do it!"

The boys all pushed on the end of the limb, and to their surprise the climbing rock moved.

"All right, Scot!" they cheered.

Ms. Grant had watched the entire scene from a distance. She stood in amazement as the boys moved the rock.

Reflection Questions

- What are the issues in this case?
- Is it a good idea to ask young children to color following a model? Why or why not?
- In what ways is Scottie different from most kindergarten students?
- How is this difference likely to impact his experiences in school? Why?
- What should Ms. Grant do to help Scottie reach his potential?

Challenge

M ark was a 12-year-old student in Mr. Carlisle's seventh-grade geography class. He was, quite frankly, a thorn in Mr. Carlisle's side. For some reason, Mark challenged just about anything Mr. Carlisle said or asked him to do. He had done the same thing last year in world history class, but in geography his behavior was more pronounced.

Mark had always enjoyed geography. His first appearance in his K–8 school's geography bee finals was in the fourth grade (the earliest grade students were allowed to compete). That year he finished in third place overall. In fifth and sixth grades, he finished in second place; both years the winners were eighth-grade students. When he was younger, he had been allowed to attend the geography bee and frequently had been amazed at the questions the finalists missed.

During a lecture regarding Central and South America, Mr. Carlisle said, "There has always been contention regarding the border between Panama and Venezuela."

"Uh, Mr. Carlisle?" responded Mark.

"Yes, Mark," sighed Mr. Carlisle.

"Panama doesn't border Venezuela."

"Well, sure it does, Mark. Look here."

Mr. Carlisle pointed to the map on the wall. His face turned bright red as he realized that Mark was right—Panama and Colombia share a border, but Panama and Venezuela do not.

"Told ya," said Mark.

The rest of the students laughed.

"Mark, leave," commanded Mr. Carlisle.

"Why? I was right. Is that a problem for you?"

"I said leave!"

Mark went to his usual spot in the hall, where he could still be seen by many of the other students. He proceeded to make faces to further entertain them.

The next day, Mark, who has allergies, needed to blow his nose during Mr. Carlisle's lecture. As he grabbed a tissue for himself, he looked at his classmates with a gleam in his eye. He then blew his nose in such a way that he sounded like an elephant trumpeting. The other students burst out laughing.

"Leave, Mark," said Mr. Carlisle.

"For blowing my nose?" Mark asked indignantly. "For crying out loud!"

"You heard me."

Mark again went to his spot in the hall and again entertained his classmates.

Later in the school year, while discussing Europe, Mr. Carlisle mentioned that Spain was isolated on the Iberian peninsula.

"Uh, Mr. Carlisle?" asked Mark.

"Yes, Mark?"

"What about Portugal?"

"What do you mean?"

"Well, you said that Spain is isolated on the Iberian peninsula, but Portugal is there, too."

"Oh, well, that hardly counts," responded Mr. Carlisle.

"What do you mean by that? I'm Portuguese! What about Magellan? Portugal does too count!"

Mr. Carlisle didn't know quite how to respond, so he just moved on with his lecture, ignoring Mark's outburst. Later, during a team meeting, he brought up Mark's behavior to the rest of the team, hoping that one of his colleagues would offer some tips on getting Mark to tone things down and behave better. "I just don't get this kid," Mr. Carlisle shared. "Quite frankly he drives me crazy—and I think he does it purposely."

"Are you talking about Mark Gomes?" asked Mrs. Carter.

"Yeah."

"Well, I can hardly believe that! I have no problem at all with him in algebra! He's a very well-behaved boy. He works hard and never gives me any lip at all."

"Well, you should see him in my class," responded Mr. Carlisle. "He is a royal pain in the butt!"

Nothing was resolved during the meeting except the fact that Mr. Carlisle and Mrs. Carter had very different experiences with Mark.

Things continued in the same fashion in Mr. Carlisle's geography class. Mark was sent out of class an average of three times per week. He didn't seem to mind in the least. In fact, it was almost as if he was trying to get sent out of class. He refused to do some of the drill and practice activities that Mr. Carlisle designed to help his students learn national capitals. He was sloppy in his map exercises, although he always earned A's on his tests. He entertained his classmates with obnoxious noises.

In early January, Mr. Carlisle's class began a unit on Africa. Mr. Carlisle distributed maps to the class. Mark looked at the map and shook his head in disgust.

"Mr. Carlisle?" he asked.

"Yeah, Mark."

"How old is this map?"

"I don't know. Why?"

"Because Zaire is on this map."

"Well, that's because Zaire is in Africa, Mark, and we're studying Africa," responded Mr. Carlisle.

"Zaire hasn't existed since 1997. It's called the Democratic Republic of Congo now. Don't you ever get new stuff? I mean, you could just download a current map from the Web."

Mr. Carlisle put his head in his hands and, with tears in his eyes, asked, "Why do you always use your brains against me?"

Mark left the classroom with a satisfied smirk on his face.

Reflection Questions

- What are the issues in this case?
- Describe the situation from Mr. Carlisle's perspective.
- Describe the situation from Mark's perspective.
- Based on the evidence in the case, at what stage of cognitive development do you believe Mark to be operating? Why?
- Why do you think Mark behaves the way he does in Mr. Carlisle's class?
- Why does he behave well in algebra?
- In what ways does Mr. Carlisle contribute to the problem?
- What could Mr. Carlisle have done differently?
- How will Mr. Carlisle's end response impact Mark's future behavior?

I Can Read!

Ms. Bluder taught second grade at a small elementary school in a rural town. She had a very diverse group of students with regard to readiness. This diversity was most pronounced in the area of reading. Some of her students were reading at the fourth-grade level. Others barely recognized letter–sound relationships. Ms. Bluder was worried about the students who were struggling with reading. She thought the ability to read at grade level was the most important thing for her students to achieve. She understood how important reading was to success in other academic areas.

Because she had several students who were struggling readers, she decided to take some action. She elicited help from community volunteers to work regularly with her struggling readers. Each day a volunteer came into the classroom and worked with each of her six struggling readers for 10 to 15 minutes. The children read to their community volunteers. The volunteers provided scaffolding for the students and valuable one-on-one attention.

One of Ms. Bluder's students who struggled with reading was Craig. At the beginning of the school year, Craig was reading at the 30th percentile nationally. Another struggling reader was Casey, who read at the 20th percentile. Both children participated in the reading volunteer program, and both made excellent progress. They both formed a bond with their Friday volunteer, Mrs. Giese.

The fourth Friday Mrs. Giese was working with the children, Casey ran to greet her as she entered the classroom. Casey gave her a huge hug, grabbed her hand, and led her to the reading corner. "Look, Mrs. Giese, look! I can read!"

"You can? That's great Casey! Show me!"

Casey sat down with Mrs. Giese and read her the book she had been working on for the past week. She stumbled over only a few words. When she was finished, she looked up at Mrs. Giese and beamed.

"That was wonderful, Casey! I'm so proud of you!" exclaimed Mrs. Giese, hugging Casey.

"Can we read another one?" asked Casey.

"We sure can, Casey. Go pick out a new book."

When the children went to PE, Mrs. Giese met with Ms. Bluder and told her about Casey's reading.

"You know, Nancy, I think what she really needs is the one on one. She doesn't seem to get a lot of attention at home," said Ms. Bluder.

"Well, I'm certainly willing to give her that," responded Mrs. Giese. "She is a really sweet kid."

While Craig was a little slower to warm up than was Casey, he and Mrs. Giese also developed a bond. Craig loved Amelia Bedelia books. To Mrs. Giese's amazement, he seemed to understand most of the double meanings in the books. "This kid is really quick," she thought. "I need to nurture this." Once again she spoke to Ms. Bluder, asking if she could bring in some special books for Craig that contained more double meanings.

"Sure," agreed Ms. Bluder. "I think he'd like that."

The next Friday, Mrs. Giese brought in several books for Craig. He was happily surprised. As he read one of the new books to Mrs. Giese, he came across a name he didn't know. "What's this word, Mrs. G?"

"Can you sound it out?" she asked.

Craig struggled a little but came up with the name—"Pringle, right?"

"That's right, Craig. Good job!"

"Hey, if her name is Mrs. Pringle, does she live in one of those little cans?" he laughed.

Mrs. Giese laughed right along with him. "I don't know, Craig. What do you think?" she asked.

"I think so." He continued to tell Mrs. Giese a story about Mrs. Pringle living in a can with her children the chips. They laughed until they had tears streaming down their faces.

Craig continued to read with Mrs. Giese on a weekly basis. By the middle of the school year, he was reading at the 75th percentile. Mrs. Giese had noticed his progress. "You don't really need my help with reading anymore, do you, Craig?" she asked.

"Don't tell!" he whispered.

"Why not?" she whispered back. "Is it a secret?"

"Yes! If Ms. Bluder knows, she might not let us read together anymore."

"Well, how about if I tell her that you're a great reader but we're having too much fun to stop and we'll just read more challenging books," offered Mrs. Giese.

"You'd do that, Mrs. G? You don't just read with kids who need you?"

"I'd do that, Craig. I like to read with kids who want to read with me."

"Thanks!" he responded with a huge grin.

Mrs. Giese spoke with Ms. Bluder and shared Craig's request.

"Of course, you two can continue to work together. Why argue with success?" she responded.

On the last day of their reading program, Mrs. Giese and Craig each brought the other a good-bye gift—a can of Pringles. They both laughed.

Casey wasn't ready to let go. "Will you read with me next year?" she asked tearfully.

"Well, Casey, I'd love to, but that's up to you and your new teacher."

Casey hugged Mrs. Giese tightly. Mrs. Giese returned the hug. "You have a good summer, Casey. Keep reading."

Reflection Questions

- What are the issues in this case?
- Explain why this reading program was so successful, tying your response to theory and research regarding literacy education.
- What does Craig's understanding of the double meanings in books mean regarding his development?
- Was it OK for Mrs. Giese to hug Casey? Why or why not?
- Was it acceptable for Mrs. Giese to continue to work with Craig although he no longer really needed her help? Why or why not?
- What will you do to ensure that your students reach their reading potential?

Mine!

Mr. Richards taught kindergarten at Roosevelt Elementary School. He enjoyed watching his students mature throughout the year. For some children the first day of school was the first time they had been with a large group of children, while for others it was old hat.

Among Mr. Richards's goals for his students was socialization. He wanted his students to leave kindergarten able to play and work cooperatively and armed with a basic understanding of the conventions that govern social behavior. To this end, he set up many situations that allowed or required his students to work and play with one another.

Much of the children's day was spent playing freely with materials and toys in the classroom while Mr. Richards observed them. He used these observations to assess social development among the children so that he could create appropriate activities to enhance this aspect of development.

One young girl, Angel, was playing in the science area with a boy, Chad. Angel was sorting rocks, while Chad was counting seeds. Chad appeared to be intrigued by the rocks she was handling. He reached across the table and picked one up in his hand.

"Mine!" shouted Angel.

Chad started at Angel's response. "Mr. Richards says we have to share," he responded without giving the rock back to Angel. He began to examine the rock.

Angel's face clouded over. "Give it back!" she yelled.

"No. I'm using it," responded Chad.

"I had it first," said Angel angrily.

"Yeah, but you weren't using it. I need it," responded Chad.

"No, I need it. It's MINE!" shouted Angel.

At this point, Mr. Richards intervened. "Angel, why don't you want to share the rocks with Chad?" he asked.

"Because I need it," she stated adamantly.

"Why do you need all the rocks, Angel?" asked Mr. Richards.

"Cuz I had them first," she responded.

"Angel, you know that we are a sharing class. We share toys and materials in this class so that everyone has a chance to use them."

"I know, but he didn't even ask—he just took it" she responded glumly, looking down at the table.

"Is there something special about this rock that makes you need it instead of another?" asked Mr. Richards.

"No," responded Angel. "I want them all so I can sort them into piles."

"I see. Well, Angel, I don't think it will ruin your sorting for Chad to use this rock, do you?"

"I guess not," Angel responded sadly.

"Chad, do you have something to say to Angel?" asked Mr. Richards.

"Angel, can I please use this rock?" asked Chad.

"Angel?" asked Mr. Richards.

"I guess."

"Chad?" prompted Mr. Richards.

"Thank you," answered Chad.

"There, that's better. You each have rocks to play with and everybody's happy," said Mr. Richards with a smile. "I'm proud of you Angel."

As Mr. Richards walked away, Angel said under her breath, "I'm not happy."

Reflection Questions

- What are the issues in this case?
- Explain the situation from Angel's perspective.
- Explain the situation from Chad's perspective.
- How well do you think Mr. Richards did in helping Chad and Angel solve their conflict? Why? What, if anything, would you have done differently?
- What developmental factors might contribute to Angel's lack of willingness to share?
- What do you think of Mr. Richards's social objectives for his class? Are they developmentally appropriate? Why or why not?

Tragedy

"**D**id you hear?" cried Louisa to her friend, Joanne. "Chris Kotter is dead!"

"Dead! What do you mean, dead?"

"I just heard on the radio that he was killed in an accident last night. Isn't it awful! I just can't believe it! He was such a great guy!" Louisa broke down in tears.

The girls were standing outside their middle school discussing the untimely death of a football player at their local high school.

"Oh my gosh, Louisa! That's terrible! What happened?" asked Joanne.

Through sobs and tears, Louisa answered, "I guess he was on his way home after going to a party last night and drove into a tree. I just can't believe this! How could he possibly be dead?"

Joanne started to cry along with Louisa. Other girls approached them to see why they were crying and hugging each other. As Louisa and Joanne shared the news, other girls began crying as well.

"Chris Kotter is dead? Oh no!"

"How could he be dead? He's only seventeen!"

The group of girls entered the school with tears streaming down their faces, red eyes, and sniffling noses. When they entered their first-hour class, their teacher, Mr. Webb, gave them an odd look.

"Girls," he asked, "is something wrong?"

"Wrong? Oh no, Mr. Webb, nothing's wrong," Louisa said, choking back sobs. "Chris Kotter died last night, that's all." Then she began to sob uncontrollably. Soon Joanne and two other girls joined her.

"You mean Chris Kotter, the varsity football player?" asked Mr. Webb.

"Y-yeah," responded Joanne.

"That's certainly a tragedy," said Mr. Webb. "Did you know him well?" he asked, assuming that he must have been a family friend of one of the girls for them to react so strongly.

"N-n-no," responded Louisa, "but I watched him play every Friday night. How could something so terrible happen?"

"Louisa, you didn't know him?" asked Mr. Webb.

"Not really."

"Did any of you other girls know him?" asked Mr. Webb.

The girls all shook their heads, but the tears kept flowing.

"Mr. Webb?" asked Louisa. "I just can't do any science today. I can't think. I'm too upset to do anything!" she said through her tears.

"Look girls, this is a terrible thing—a young man has died. But you didn't know him. Your only contact with him was watching him play football. You have to control your emotions," advised Mr. Webb.

"Oh, you just don't understand!" yelled Louisa. "This is the worst thing that's ever happened to me!"

"But Louisa, it didn't happen to you, or to Joanne, or to any of you girls. It happened to Chris Kotter and his family and friends," responded Mr. Webb. "Now calm down and let's get down to business."

Louisa looked at Mr. Webb in shock. "You just don't get it! You don't understand at all!" she yelled. She ran out of the classroom.

Joanne followed on her heels, crying the whole way. Following them, three other girls left in tears. Meanwhile, Mr. Webb stood staring after them and wondering how on earth they could be so upset by the death of someone they didn't even know.

Reflection Questions

- What are the issues in this case?
- Explain the situation from Louisa's and Joanne's perspectives.
- Explain the situation from Mr. Webb's perspective.
- What developmental factors contributed to the girls' reaction to Chris Kotter's death?
- What do you think of the way Mr. Webb handled the situation? Why?
- What, if anything, would you do differently?

Depressed?

A aron was a sophomore at West High School. He was a nice, quiet boy who earned mostly C's and D's in his college preparatory coursework. The one exception was English, in which he earned A's and B's. This might be attributed to the new English teacher at West—Mr. Byron. Mr. Byron's teaching techniques weren't like those of most of the other teachers. He didn't lecture much. Instead, the students spent the bulk of their class time writing or discussing the assigned reading material. He was a popular teacher. Students in his classes were very motivated, and most did well.

Aaron did not participate in extracurricular activities. When he was younger, he had been an athlete, but a serious illness during fifth grade left him with some physical limitations that made playing sports difficult for him. He continued to try sports for two years, but it was obvious that he was no longer competitive athletically. He had always socialized with members of his teams. He tried to continue these relationships but found that he no longer had much in common with his former teammates. They were always busy with practices and games. He spent most of his time alone playing video games—something at which he excelled.

Aaron began missing school on a fairly regular basis, complaining of headaches and stomachaches.

"Mom, please let me stay home. I don't feel good," he implored one day.

"Aaron, you've missed a lot of school already."

"I know. But, Mom, I *hate* school! It's boring and pointless."

"Honey, it's not pointless. You need to go."

That day, during English class, Aaron started crying.

"Aaron, are you OK?" asked Mr. Byron.

"I feel like crap, Mr. B."

"OK, go to the office and get permission to go home. We'll see you when you feel better."

Aaron called his mother, who came to pick him up. When he got into the car, he started crying. "Honey, what is it?" she asked.

"I just hate school so much, Mom! Please don't make me go back," Aaron cried.

"Aaron, honey, you can't drop out of school."

"I wish I was dead," responded Aaron quietly.

Aaron spent the afternoon in his room playing video games. His mother called the school counselor, Connie Kreider. "I'm really worried about him, Connie. He hates school, wants to drop out. He's sick all the time. He's crying. He doesn't eat. I'm really worried. Would you please ask his teachers if they've noticed anything?"

"Sure, Sharon. I'll talk to each of them today. I personally haven't noticed anything, but I don't see him very often. When he comes back, I'll make it a point to keep tabs on him."

"Thanks, Connie, I really appreciate it!" responded Aaron's mother.

Connie sent a note to each of Aaron's teachers advising them of Sharon's concerns and requesting that they let her know about any unusual behavior on Aaron's part. The only teacher who had noticed anything was Mr. Byron. According to Mr. Byron, Aaron just seemed as if he didn't feel very well and hadn't for some time.

"He's a really good kid. I like him, Connie. But he's always sick. I think he's had every virus that's gone around the school this year. I think that's probably it."

Connie reported back to Aaron's mother that while his teachers were concerned about his absences, they hadn't noticed anything terribly unusual—just that Aaron didn't seem to feel well.

Sharon took Aaron to the doctor, who ran tests for mononucleosis, strep throat, and anemia. All the tests were negative. The only thing of note was that Aaron had lost 5 pounds since his last physical.

"Aaron, I don't know what to tell you, kiddo. The doc says you're OK. You really need to go to school."

Aaron looked at his mother with tears in his eyes. "Please, Mom, don't make me go. I don't feel good."

"Aaron, is somebody picking on you at school?"

"No, Mom. I just don't feel good."

Sharon allowed Aaron to stay home for the rest of the day but insisted that he go to school the next day. While she was doing laundry, she noticed a piece of notebook paper in one of Aaron's pants pockets. She unfolded it and read it. She was shocked. It was a draft of a poem about death and dying that Aaron had written. He had marked all over it to make changes. It was very dark and disturbing.

While Aaron's mother was doing laundry, Aaron was in Mr. Byron's English class. He acted as if he felt much better. He was even laughing with some of the other students. Aaron stayed back when Mr. Byron dismissed the class. "Hey, Mr. B. I just want to thank you for being so cool about me being sick and everything."

"No problem, Aaron. It's nice to see you feeling better!"

"Well, thanks again. I just wanted to give you this." Aaron handed Mr. Byron his autographed football.

"Hey, Aaron, you shouldn't be giving me this. This is something you should hang onto."

"Nah, I don't need it. I want you to have it. Bye." Aaron turned and walked out of the room, leaving Mr. Byron stunned.

Reflection Questions

- What are the issues in this case?
- What do you think is going on with Aaron? Why?
- What should Mr. Byron do at this point? Why?
- What, if anything, should Aaron's mother have done differently? Why?

Who Am I Now?

Ken was a fifth-grade student at Hauser Elementary School. He was an active young man who participated in soccer, basketball, and baseball. He swam, he golfed, and he rode his bicycle everywhere his parents would allow him. Ken was very popular with his classmates and teammates alike because of his quick wit, ready smile, and congenial personality. In short, he was a great kid.

During a soccer game in October, Ken was taken down from behind by an opposing player. Unlike on most occasions, this time Ken did not get up. He was writhing in pain. The coach came out on the field, took one look at Ken's leg, and called his parents onto the field. Ken's dad called an ambulance, and the game was suspended until Ken was carried off the field on a stretcher. When Ken got to the emergency room, the doctor set his obviously broken leg. However, some other things disturbed the doctor, and Ken was admitted for observation and tests—including several blood tests.

The next day, Ken's parents received very bad news. Ken had leukemia. This was the reason his leg had broken as easily as it had. It also explained Ken's fatigue of late, something his mother had blamed on too many soccer practices. Ken's parents understandably were devastated. Telling Ken was the hardest thing they had ever done. They had to remain upbeat even though they were scared out of their minds. They didn't want Ken to share their fear.

Ken's parents alerted the school to Ken's illness as soon as they could. They asked that Ken's teacher, Mr. Bastian, share the news with the class. Mr. Bastian pondered how to tell a group of 10- and 11-year-old students that their classmate, of whom they were all fond, had cancer.

"Class, I have some bad news," he started. "Ken has leukemia. He'll be in the hospital for quite a while, and then he'll be at home. He won't be back to school for at least a couple of months."

"Is he gonna die, Mr. Bastian?" asked Peter.

"I hope not, Peter, but I won't lie to you. We don't really know for sure."

"What are they gonna do to him in the hospital?" asked John.

"He'll get lots of medicine. He might get a bone marrow transplant. Ken has really good doctors, and they'll do their best to help him get well."

"Can we make him get well cards?" asked Toni.

"Sure we can. Why don't we do that now? I'm sure it will make him feel better to know we're all thinking of him."

The class made get well cards for Ken—not just that day, but once a week until he was able to return to school. Many of the cards had pictures drawn on them of Ken playing soccer or basketball, along with wishes for a speedy recovery.

Ken responded well to treatment, but it left him weak and bald. He stayed out of school for over two months. When his doctor told him he could return to school, Ken was worried. He couldn't do anything—no PE, no soccer, no basketball. He was skinny—and bald! To make matters worse, the school had a "no hat" rule.

Ken's parents spoke to the principal and to Mr. Bastian. Both agreed that Ken could wear a hat to school if he chose. Mr. Bastian promised to tell the other students what to expect.

"Kids, Ken is coming back to school on Monday. You should know that he's lost quite a bit of weight. It'll be a while before he can join you on the basketball court, so cut him some slack, OK? Oh, yeah, I almost forgot. The chemotherapy made Ken's hair fall out, so we're suspending the no-hat rule. Ken can wear hats and so can you guys, if you want."

"You mean Ken's bald, Mr. Bastian?" asked Peter.

"That's exactly what I mean, Peter. Please don't make fun of him, OK?"

"We wouldn't do that, Mr. Bastian."

"Well, see that you don't."

On Monday morning, Ken was nervous. His parents tried to calm him and assure him that everything would be fine. Ken arrived at school on time, but all his classmates were already in their classroom. They had hung balloons and streamers all over the room, along with signs that said "Welcome Back Ken! We Missed You!" Ken's jaw dropped when he saw the room. He broke into a smile. The smile turned into a laugh as he looked at his classmates. All the boys had shaved their heads—even Mr. Bastian! They were all as bald as he was. "You guys are the best!" said Ken.

They had a fine time that morning, but Ken was very tired when he left at noon. He slept most of the afternoon. The next day, it was back to business as usual—except for all the bald heads. Ken worked hard trying to catch up with the class, and he had a lot of catching up to do. Because Ken was back at school, infection was no longer a serious issue. He invited several of his classmates to his house over the weekend to play video games.

"Sorry, man, I can't," replied Peter. Soccer practice starts this weekend. We're moving up a division, so coach wants to start early."

"Oh. OK"

Ken spent most of the weekend alone, catching up on schoolwork and playing video games. On Sunday, Toni stopped over for a little while. She brought Ken a new hat and played a couple of video games with him before leaving. The next weekend, even Toni didn't stop by.

Ken was frustrated. He went to watch his teammates play their first soccer game, but after they won, they barely noticed his congratulations. They went off to celebrate at the nearest ice cream parlor without inviting him to join them.

Reflection Questions

- What are the issues in this case?
- Describe the situation from Ken's perspective.
- Describe the situation from his classmates' perspectives.
- Was it a good idea for the males in Ken's class to shave their heads? Why or why not?
- What struggles is Ken having with regard to his identity development?
- Why did most of his classmates not visit Ken once they were allowed to?
- How do you anticipate Ken will adjust to his new peer status?
- How can Ken's teacher and coach help?

Pants

E leven-year-old Nathan and his mother were shopping for new clothes because Nathan had outgrown most of those in his closet. They were in their sixth store at the mall, and Nathan's mom was getting tired of hearing everything that was wrong with the clothes she suggested to Nathan.

"OK, Nate, I'm done. You pick something," she said.

"No problem. I know just where to go," responded Nathan.

He hurried off to another store with his mother in tow. Nathan's mom was surprised by the store to which he had taken her. Loud music was playing, and lights were flashing. The staff was dressed in what she considered to be odd clothing. Nathan nearly sprinted to the back of the store and returned with a pair of red, faux-leather pants.

"You're kidding, right, Nathan?" asked his mother.

"No. Wait till you see them on, Mom. They're awesome!"

Nathan went into the dressing room to try on the pants. His mother stood outside the dressing room, shaking her head and chuckling. "Kids," she thought, "you never know what they'll come up with."

When Nathan came out of the dressing room, he was wearing the red, faux-leather pants. His mother was shocked to see that they only went down to the top of his calves and were skin tight. Nathan was all smiles. "Aren't they great, Mom?" he exclaimed.

"Well, they're different, Nate, I'll give them that."

"Can I have them, Mom? Please? These are sooooooo cool!"

"Nathan, they look like Capri pants. And they're so tight," his mother responded.

"Mom, these are just like the pants we saw that guy wearing at the concert the other night. Please?"

"OK, Nate. You can have them," his mother acquiesced.

The next day, Nathan was excited to wear his new pants to school. He wanted all his friends to see how cool he looked in them. He practically strutted as he left his mom's car and walked up to join his friends at the entrance to the school. "Hey, guys. What's up?" he said.

"Dang, Nate, what's with the pants?" asked Paul.

"Aren't they cool?" asked Nathan. "I got them last night." Nathan turned around in a circle so his friends would see his new pants from all angles.

"Cool?" responded Casey. "They look like girls' pants!"

"Yeah," agreed Landon. "You're not thinkin' of havin' an operation or anything, are you?" he asked with a grin.

"What?" responded Nathan. "You don't think they're cool? Come on, they're just like the ones what's-his-name was wearing the other night at the concert."

"Yeah, dude, they are. But that guy bats for the other team, you know what I mean?" said Casey.

"Huh?"

"Come on, Nate. Those pants are not exactly what we'd call manly, ya know," said Paul.

"What do you mean by that?" asked Nathan.

"Nate. Lose the pants before you lose your friends and some guy decides to make you his girlfriend," said Landon.

Nathan was shocked by his friends' reactions to his new pants. He thought they would think the pants were really cool. They all liked the singer who had worn some just like them at the concert. Suddenly, he felt very uncomfortable in the red pants. Instead of going to his first class, he went to the office.

"I don't feel so good," he said to the school secretary.

"Are you sure, Nathan? You just got here."

"I'm sure, Mrs. Bish. Can you call my mom?"

Mrs. Bish called Nathan's mom, who came to pick him up and take him home. By the time they got there, Nathan was in tears. How could he have made such a mistake?

Reflection Questions

- What are the issues in this case?
- Explain the situation from Nathan's perspective.
- Explain the situation from the perspective of Nathan's friends.
- What functions of friendship were evident in this case?
- Explain the importance of clothes to young adolescents, taking into consideration issues of the functions of friendship, peer acceptance, clique and crowd formation, and identity development.
- Should Nathan's mother have allowed him to purchase the pants? Why or why not?
- How do you think this is likely to impact Nathan socially?

(Almost) All Grown Up, Now Where Do I Go?

Christina was a senior in high school. She would graduate in a few months among the top 10 students in her class of 550. All of her friends were talking about what colleges they planned to attend and what subjects they would major in. Christina, however, had no idea what she wanted to do with her life.

Christina's parents were both college-educated. They had always assumed that Christina would attend college. After all, she was a very bright girl who excelled at academics, and college had always been an expectation. They took Christina to visit several college campuses in hopes that one would spark her interest. Christina's reactions were lukewarm at best. She didn't like the idea of sharing a small dorm room with another girl she didn't even know, and she was uncertain of her ability to learn in large lecture classes.

Christina's favorite teacher was her social sciences teacher, Mr. Welch. She had been in both his American history course and his American government course. She had earned full possible points in both courses and had impressed Mr. Welch with her insight and analytical thinking ability. He often complimented her on her work and even shared her work with other teachers. "You should read Christina's paper. Look at this title: 'The Moral Implications of the Scarlet Letter on the Puritan Society'! Have you ever seen anything like this out of a high school student?"

Because of their shared interests and Christina's exemplary work, Mr. Welch and Christina formed a bond. When Christina needed a nonparent adult to talk with, Mr. Welch was the person to whom she turned. Mr. Welch encouraged Christina to explore career options and spoke often of the fun and excitement of attending college. However, Christina remained unsure of what path to take. When Mr. Welch thought he had done all he could to help Christina explore her options, he sought help for her from one of the school's guidance counselors, Mr. Roberts.

"What do you mean you're not sure about college, Christina?" Mr. Roberts asked.

"I don't know, Mr. Roberts. I'm just so sick of school. I've been in school since I was five. I'm tired of it. I think I'm ready to be a real grown-up. You know, get a job, an apartment, and all that," responded Christina.

"What kind of job do you think you can get? Do you want to work in a factory? Do you want to sell trendy clothes?"

"Well, I've done some retail. I kind of liked it. I wouldn't mind business, either."

"You would be bored out of your mind doing the kinds of jobs you could get without a college degree, Christina. You're really bright. You belong in college!"

"Do I, Mr. Roberts? I think it would be a waste of money. I don't know what I want to do. How can I go to school if I don't have a goal?"

Mr. Roberts arranged to take Christina to every career exploration activity in the area. He took her to a career fair at a local hospital, where they discussed various health-care careers such as physical therapy, nursing, medicine, and radiology. Christina was uninspired. He pulled her out of class to attend a career expo in a nearby large city. Here Christina explored all sorts of options—teaching, psychology, counseling, social work, business, accounting, and many other fields.

"Well, what do you think, Christina?" asked Mr. Roberts.

"I don't know. Everything except for accounting seems like it could be fun. But I'm just not ready to make a decision and commit the rest of my life to it, you know. It's just overwhelming."

"Christina, you have to decide on a school soon or you won't get in at all," said Mr. Roberts.

"I know. I know. But I can't decide."

"Look, pick a school. Take your general education courses and decide on a major later."

"That seems like a waste of time and money, Mr. Roberts. I think I'll just take some time off and work. Maybe get married or something," responded Christina.

"Married! What are you talking about?"

"Well, we've been going out for a long time, Mr. Roberts. We just might."

Exasperated, Mr. Roberts took Christina back to school. He had a meeting with Mr. Welch. "I've tried, Paul. I really have," said Mr. Roberts. "She has no interest in anything we've seen. No, I take that back. She's interested in lots of things, but not interested enough in any of them—except that boyfriend of hers."

"I was afraid that might be part of the problem. Keep trying, OK?"

"Argh. I don't know how many more of these things I can drag her to."

"Well, she keeps agreeing to go, right? As long as she does that, there's hope."

Reflection Questions

- What are the issues in this case?
- Explain the situation from Christina's perspective.
- Explain the situation from Mr. Welch's and Mr. Roberts's perspectives.
- Explain Christina's situation using Marcia's theory of identity development.
- What would Erikson say about Christina?
- What cultural factors might be influencing Christina?
- Should Christina go to college now? Why or why not?

Dolls and Soldiers

Ms. Benton teaches kindergarten at Cross Elementary School. Her classroom is divided into several play centers. One area contains cars and trucks. An adjacent area contains various building materials, such as wood and plastic blocks. The science area has shells, rocks, magnets, leaves, and pods. Another area contains a miniature kitchen, dolls, and doll beds. Adjacent to that is a trunk filled with "dress-up" clothes for role playing. Still another area has books and puzzles. Finally, one corner houses two computers, tablets of paper, and crayons.

During a large portion of their day, Ms. Benton's students are allowed to play freely in any area of the room they like. She makes no effort to control their choices. Rather, they choose what they want to do, and she observes their play. She takes careful notes of her observations, which she uses to make inferences regarding her students' cognitive and social development. She intervenes only when she is asked or to stop a physical altercation.

Ms. Benton has noticed over the years that her students' behavior patterns are fairly consistent across classes. Generally, the boys spend their free time building, playing with the trucks, or engaging in role playing in which they are soldiers, police officers, fire fighters, or superheroes. The girls, on the other hand, tend to spend their time playing with the dolls and dressing up for their role-play that involves either family life or glamour. Even when the children seem to be engaged in nonstereotypical play, a more careful observation often yields conflicting information. For instance, one day Ms. Benton observed Joshua in the doll center. Thinking that perhaps he was going to allow his nurturing side to emerge, she moved closer to observe the interactions.

"Don't worry, children, I'll save you!" Joshua said to the other students.

"Thank you, Superman!" said Claire.

Ms. Benton smiled. "Well, I was only a little off," she thought. Later she observed Joshua with a small block in his hand pretending to shoot another boy who was invading the house area through a pretend window. "Definitely a little off," she chuckled.

Ms. Benton also observed Suzie playing with the cars and trucks in the sandbox. Because this was out of the ordinary for Suzie, she decided to observe her more closely. As she approached her, Ms. Benton listened to what Suzie was saying.

"OK, now turn left, honey. We need to pick up Johnny at soccer practice."

Ms. Benton smiled. Suzie had two blocks in the toy car and had set up several others in another part of the sandbox. She was pretending they were a family.

Of course, this wasn't always the case. Every now and then students truly would cross over into the traditional realm of the opposite gender. Billy, for instance, seemed to enjoy playing with the kitchen set. He often "cooked" fake food to serve to the other children. Sometimes he set up a "concession stand" for the construction workers in the building area and served food there as well. The girls accepted Billy into their world easily, but some of the boys told him that he engaged in "girl stuff." He seemed to take this in stride and told them that cooking was "man stuff." Billy's father was a chef.

Crystal loved to build towers and houses out of different materials—blocks, plastic bricks, logs, even rocks. Some of her buildings were quite elaborate. She obviously took great care in building them. The only problem she ever had with other children in the building area was when they knocked down her buildings. When that happened she became very angry.

Reflection Questions

- What are the issues in this case?
- How would a social-cognitive theorist explain the sex-stereotypical behavior of the children in this case?
- How would a biological theorist explain the sex-stereotypical behavior of the children in this case?
- How do you think engaging in gender-atypical behavior will impact Billy and Crystal socially?
- Will the impact be the same for both of them? Why or why not?
- What aspect of physical development is displayed in Crystal's building ability?
- What would Howard Gardner say about Crystal's building ability?
- What would Piaget say about Ms. Benton's belief that young children should spend a large portion of their day engaged in free play? Do you agree? Why or why not?
- Do you agree with Ms. Benton that observing young children is a good way to learn about their development? Why or why not?
- Some schools disallow playing soldier and superhero. Why do you suppose they do this? What are the pros and cons of this practice?

Hallway Horseplay

Tim and Demarcus are eighth-grade students at Columbus Middle School. They have been best friends since they were in kindergarten. Both boys are athletic and participate in school sports. Neither has been in any serious trouble at school. They have each had the occasional detention, usually for boisterous behavior. They frequently have served these detentions together because their infractions occurred together. They are friendly boys and are well liked by both the other students in their classes and their teachers.

One day, after a particularly grueling algebra exam, the boys were on their way to science class.

"Hey Demarcus, how bad did you flunk that test?" joked Tim.

"Me? I aced that sucker! How bad did you do?" retorted Demarcus.

"I ain't never failed a test in my life!"

"Yeah, except for maybe English. Listen to yourself!" laughed Demarcus.

Tim pushed Demarcus in the shoulder, causing Demarcus to drop his books. While the books went flying, Tim started laughing. Demarcus joined Tim in his laughter. "Oh man, you are gonna wish you hadn't done that, Timmy-boy!" he threatened with laughter and a twinkle in his eye.

"Yeah, right. What you gonna do about it, Demi?" laughed Tim.

"Demi! Did you just call me Demi? You are gonna PAY!"

With that, Demarcus shoved Tim. Tim pushed back harder. Both boys continued to laugh and to trade insults and shoves. The force escalated with each shove until at one point Tim pushed Demarcus hard enough to send him flying across the hallway into the lockers on the other side.

"Got you good, Demi!" laughed Tim.

When Demarcus turned around, he was bleeding from his mouth.

"Oh shit. You OK, dude?" asked Tim. "I didn't mean to hurt you!"

"Yeah, I'm OK, but damn, Timmy, don't push so hard! That hurt."

Just then Mr. Kotter, the boys' algebra teacher, intervened. "What is wrong with you two? Knock it off! Head on down to the office! NOW!"

Tim helped Demarcus up and gave him a tissue for his mouth. "Uh-oh, dude, we got a problem," he said with fear in his voice.

"What's that?" responded Demarcus. "You afraid they're gonna call your mommy?"

"No, they're definitely gonna call both our parents! Your front tooth is half gone!"

"Oh man! My parents are gonna kill me. You too!"

The boys walked to the office with their heads down, far more worried about Demarcus's tooth than they were about the punishment they would receive.

Ms. Broadhouse, the dean of students, met them at the door. "Mr. Kotter told me you were coming, boys. Explain yourselves."

Demarcus let Tim do the talking. "We were just goofin' around, Ms. Broadhouse. It was no big deal."

"Boys, fighting is indeed a big deal," responded Ms. Broadhouse.

"That's just it, Ms. Broadhouse, we weren't fighting. Demarcus is my best friend. We were just playing. It got out of hand. We're sorry. It won't happen again."

"Demarcus, what do you have to say for yourself?" asked Ms. Broadhouse.

Demarcus looked first at Ms. Broadhouse, then at Tim.

"Well? I'm waiting."

"We were just goofing around. No big deal," said Demarcus softly.

"Oh my God! Look at your tooth! Both of you sit down right now. I'm calling your parents. You are suspended, Tim. Ten days. Three days for you, Demarcus."

The boys were stunned. "But Ms. Broadhouse," began Tim.

"Tim shouldn't get any more punishment than me," said Demarcus.

Reflection Questions

- What are the issues in this case?
- Describe the situation from Tim's and Demarcus's perspectives.
- Describe the situation from Ms. Broadhouse's perspective.
- Is the behavior of Tim and Demarcus typical of young adolescent males?
- What functions of friendship are evident in the case?
- Why did Demarcus initially allow Tim to do the talking?
- Is a 10-day suspension for Tim warranted? Why or why not?
- Would your feelings be different if Demarcus had not broken his tooth?
- Do the boys deserve the same punishment, as Demarcus suggested? Why or why not?
- Demarcus's family does not have dental insurance. Should Tim's family pay Demarcus's dental bill? Why or why not?

Communication

J ake and Jenny were seniors in high school and had been dating for over a year. While they had a good relationship, like most young couples they had their complaints about each other. They often discussed these complaints with their friends.

"I don't understand Jake sometimes," complained Jenny. "When I call him to talk, he always wants to know what I want and tries to get off the phone as fast as possible. I really call him just to talk."

"I have the same problem with Ben," replied Jenny's friend Maya.

"Why don't they ever just want to talk? I could talk for hours."

"Yeah, me too. With Ben, it's all business. When should he pick me up? Does he need to wear anything special? What time am I supposed to be home?"

"That sounds just like Jake. Exactly," said Jenny. "His idea of a phone call is 15 seconds. I'd rather talk for like 15 minutes. And you know what else?"

"What?"

"Every time I have a problem, he tries to fix it."

"Him too?" laughed Maya. "I wonder why they do that."

"I know. I just want him to listen to me and let me figure it out. You know, like a sounding board. But no—Mr. Fix-it has to step in and solve my problem for me. It's not like I ask him to do it. He just does it!"

Jake and Ben were playing video games one Saturday and discussing their girlfriends. "You ever notice that girls don't play video games?" asked Ben.

"Yeah, Jenny hates them, and I can see why. She's terrible at them," laughed Jake.

"And how about the time they spend on the phone? You'd think their ears would get sore or something."

"If Jenny talked on the phone any more, her ear wouldn't just be sore, it'd fall off!"

The boys continued their game. At the next break in action, they continued their discussion of their girlfriends' faults. "Does Maya do that thing where she tells you about a problem she's having and then, when you tell her how to solve it, she gets all huffy and says you never just want to listen to her?" asked Jake.

"Yeah, what's up with that?" responded Ben. "You fix it for them and then they get mad!" he laughed. "Girls!"

"The worst, though, is when you call them to see if they want to do anything that night. I mean, I call you to see what you're doing, and we make plans in like 30 seconds tops, right?" said Jake.

"Yep."

"Jenny just can't get to the point. She wants to talk for like half an hour or something. It's crazy! I just don't have that much to say. And then she's mad cuz I'm not participating."

"Or worse yet, Maya says I'm not listening," said Ben.

"Well, are you?" laughed Jake.

"Well, for a little while. But before long I'm kinda zoned out watching TV or something. How can I listen for that long?"

Reflection Questions

- What are the issues in this case?
- What do we call Jake's style of communication? Is this typical of males?
- What do we call Jenny's style of communication? Is this typical of females?
- What do adolescents need to know about gender differences in communication? Why?
- What would help adolescents communicate better across genders?

You're Gonna Get in Trouble!

Sara and Debbie were kindergarten students and best friends. They spent most of their school day together, unless Ms. Ronaldo separated them. This didn't happen often, because the girls generally were well behaved. Ms. Ronaldo required her students to clean up after themselves. If a student had been playing with the blocks, for instance, he or she needed to put them away before moving on to another activity. At the beginning of the school year, this was a problem for many of the children. They simply didn't want to take time out to put things away. Ms. Ronaldo gently reminded them of her rule when she saw children leaving a mess. She thought that taking personal responsibility for one's actions was very important.

The class had other rules, too. Students were to keep their hands, feet, and objects to themselves. They were to share the toys. They were to walk in the classroom. They were to use their inside voices. Finally, they were to treat their classmates the way they would like to be treated. These rules were established the first day of class.

One day Sara and Debbie were working in the art center. They had been painting with water-based paints on each side of the easel. After they finished admiring each other's paintings, they started cleaning up. As Debbie was putting away the red paint, she tripped and spilled it on the floor.

"Oh, you're gonna get in trouble," said Sara in a sing-song voice.

Debbie looked ready to cry. "What do you mean?" she asked.

"Look at the mess you made, Debbie!" said Sara. "There's no way you can clean that up. Ms. Ronaldo is gonna be mad!"

Debbie's lip started to tremble. Her eyes welled with tears. Soon they were rolling down her face.

"What's wrong, Debbie?" asked Ms. Ronaldo.

Debbie pointed to the paint on the floor. "I'm sorry, Ms. Ronaldo," she sobbed. "I made a big mess and I don't know how to clean it up."

"Well, Debbie, that certainly is a mess," responded Ms. Ronaldo. "Did you purposely pour the paint on the floor?"

Sara looked at Debbie and smirked.

"N-no," stammered Debbie.

"Was it an accident, Debbie?"

"Yes, it was an accident. I didn't mean to do it," answered Debbie.

"Well, these things happen," explained Ms. Ronaldo. "It looks as if you got some of it on yourself, too."

Debbie looked down at her shirt and started crying even louder.

"Debbie, it's OK. Help me get this cleaned up."

"But my shirt . . . ," Debbie sobbed.

"I'm sure your mom will understand, Sweetie. Accidents happen, and this paint will wash right out."

Ms. Ronaldo squeezed Debbie's shoulder. "Do you have extra clothes in your cubbie?"

"Yes."

"Well, go change your shirt and put that one in a bag. Then come back and we'll clean up this mess together, OK?"

Debbie gave a tentative smile. "OK, Ms. Ronaldo," she said as she went to change.

By the time Debbie had on a clean shirt, Ms. Ronaldo had gathered cleaning supplies. The pair had the floor cleaned up in short order. "OK, Debbie, you can go play now," said Ms. Ronaldo.

Debbie smiled and joined Sara at the science table. "Did you get in trouble?" asked Sara.

"No," responded Debbie.

"Why not? We're not supposed to make messes!" stated Sara.

"Ms. Ronaldo said it was an accident," answered Debbie.

"You mean if it's an accident we don't get in trouble?" asked Sara, amazed.

"I don't know. I guess."

Reflection Questions

- What are the issues in this case?
- Why do the girls assume they will get in trouble for an accident? Tie your answer to moral development.
- What do you think of Ms. Ronaldo's response to the situation? Why?
- What do you think of Ms. Ronaldo's classroom rules? Why?
- Are Ms. Ronaldo's rules developmentally appropriate?
- What do you think is the best way to establish classroom rules? Why?

I Told You!

At the beginning of the school year at Kennedy Elementary School, all the children meet in the gym for an assembly. At the assembly, the principal, Ms. Boerke, tells the children "This is a telling school." What she means is that if someone harms another student in any way, or threatens to do so, the teachers want to know about it so the situation will not escalate. Some of the children groan in response; others appear happy at the news.

Mrs. Lofton teaches fourth grade at Kennedy. This year she has a rather unruly group of students, much more difficult to manage than classes in the past. She's not sure why; individually, they are all nice children. As a group, however, they are a handful—especially the boys. They often call each other unkind names and engage in very physical play at recess. Sometimes this physical play escalates to fighting.

Jaime, one of her more difficult students, is very bright, very active, very physical, and very loud. He knows the answer to almost every question she asks in class and often shouts out his answer instead of raising his hand, preventing others from answering. In addition, he often corrects Mrs. Lofton when she misspeaks or does something incorrectly. He finishes his work quickly, but when he is done he rarely engages in anything constructive. Instead, he talks to the students around him, distracting them from their work. He appears to be a leader among his peers. If Jaime doesn't like somebody, neither will a sizable portion of the other boys in the class. If Jaime acts out in class, others soon follow suit. In a nutshell, he drives Mrs. Lofton just a little bit nuts.

One day during a morning recess basketball game, another boy, Sean, commits what Jaime considers to be a heinous foul against him. Mrs. Lofton is refereeing the game, but basketball is not her area of expertise; therefore, she does not call Sean for the foul. After picking himself up off the blacktop, Jaime complains to Mrs. Lofton about the foul, but she tells him to "just keep playing and stop whining about every little thing." Jaime rejoins the game after giving Mrs. Lofton a dirty look.

As the game gets under way again, Sean sneers at Jaime and says "Wuss!"

Jaime glares at Sean but keeps playing. The boys continue to play a very physical game, fouling each other very hard when they think they can get away with it.

A similar pattern commences during noon recess. In the final seconds of the game, Sean commits a hard foul against Jaime while Jaime is shooting to take the lead. Mrs. Lofton does not call the foul.

"Come on, Mrs. Lofton! That was really cheap! How can you let that kind of crap go?" shouts Jaime.

"Watch your language, Jaime," Mrs. Lofton responds. "Time to go in."

On the way into the school, Sean says to Jaime, "You're just ticked cuz your team sucks and I'm better than you!"

"Back off, Sean!" retorts Jaime.

During the first part of the afternoon, Sean continues to make comments to Jaime about losing the game. Jaime is determined that his team will not lose again.

When afternoon recess comes, the boys again play basketball. Once again, few fouls are called, and the play becomes quite physical. As the boys count the seconds until the whistle ending recess, Jaime's team leads by one point. Sean has the ball and is dribbling down the court. Jaime decides he cannot allow Sean to score. He fouls Sean as he shoots, causing him to miss the shot. Mrs. Lofton does not call the foul.

Sean is visibly upset when the whistle blows to end recess. On the way into the school, he hits Jaime and threatens to beat him up after school. Jaime starts to push Sean. Then he remembers that he is supposed to tell the teachers when this kind of thing happens. He restrains himself and dutifully reports to Mrs. Lofton at the next opportunity.

"Mrs. Lofton?"

"Yes, Jaime?"

"On the way in from recess, Sean hit me and said he was gonna beat me up after school."

"Oh, Jaime, what is it with you two? Get back to work. I'll take care of it."

Jaime goes back to his desk and begins working on his math homework. Mrs. Lofton calls Sean up to her desk and talks to him for a few seconds. Sean smiles at Jaime as he walks back to his seat.

After school, as Sean and Jaime are leaving the building, Sean says, "You are such a wuss, Jaime. I'm gonna kick your butt!"

Jaime is surprised. He was sure that Sean would be staying after school that day or that there would be some consequence for Sean's having hit him. Sean then hits Jaime. Jaime, frustrated and angry, punches Sean in the face, causing his nose to bleed profusely. As a stunned Sean covers his nose with his hands, blood pours from between his fingers. Jaime lands several more punches before a teacher can reach the boys and break up the fight. The teacher takes the boys to the office.

Mrs. Lofton steps into the office shaking her head. "Jaime, look what you've done to Sean. I just don't understand you!"

"But Mrs. Lofton, he hit me first, and I told you he hit me this afternoon and you didn't do anything!" replies Jaime.

"I did, Jaime. I talked to Sean and he said it wouldn't happen again."

Reflection Questions

- What are the issues in this case?
- What is Mrs. Lofton's perspective of what occurred?
- What is Sean's perspective of what occurred?
- What is Jaime's perspective of what occurred?
- What perspective of morality does Mrs. Lofton take?
- What perspective of morality does Jaime take?
- In what way does this difference in perspectives cause problems?
- At which of Kohlberg's stages of moral development do you believe Jaime to be operating? Why?
- How could this situation have been avoided?
- What should happen now? Why?

Rules and Consequences

Jamaal was an eighth-grade student at Brady Middle School. He had always been a challenging child to have in class. He was bright, curious, and very active. He rarely accepted things at face value. His elementary teachers had often referred to him as "a handful." Since entering middle school, Jamaal seemed to enjoy challenging his teachers, particularly with regard to rules for which he saw no real purpose. For instance, he often wore his hat into the school and had to be told to remove it.

During his eighth-grade year, Jamaal began to chew gum in school, in spite of the rule forbidding it. According to the student handbook that he and his mother acknowledged reading and understanding, chewing gum would result in a warning for a first offense. Each subsequent offense was punishable by a detention. After three detentions, a student would be ineligible to participate in co-curricular activities such as sports, dances, and field trips for the remainder of the quarter in which the infractions took place. Students started each quarter with a clean slate.

Jamaal was caught chewing gum five times during the first week of school. His teachers gave him the required warning, followed by four detentions, which Jamaal served—though not happily. On the day of the fourth detention, Jamaal decided to go talk to his homeroom teacher and advisor, Mrs. Cragan.

"I just don't get it, Mrs. Cragan. What's so bad about chewing gum? I mean, I don't hurt anybody. I don't blow bubbles or crack it. And I don't stick it under the desks. I just chew it."

"Jamaal, you know the rules," replied Mrs. Cragan. "Chewing gum is against school policy. You and your mom signed the rules acknowledgment. End of story."

"This is nuts!" exclaimed Jamaal. "Absolutely crazy! I'm not hurting anybody, including myself—it's sugarless."

"Jamaal, that's not the issue. You broke a rule. You keep breaking it. You know that I have to declare you ineligible for co-curriculars."

"Soccer?!" cried Jamaal.

"Yes, soccer. And dances, field trips, and clubs, too."

"This just sucks!"

"You knew the consequences and you still broke the rule. That's final."

Jamaal went home and told his mother everything that had happened. His mother was very upset. She called Mrs. Cragan to see if they would consider giving Jamaal another chance. Mrs. Cragan denied her request.

Jamaal continued chewing gum in class. His teachers decided to try another approach. They called Jamaal to one of their team planning meetings, which included all eight teachers on their middle-school team. They each told Jamaal to stop chewing gum. Jamaal sat silently during the meeting. When it was over, he simply went to class. While he didn't get caught, he chewed gum during that class.

When Jamaal told his friends about the meeting, they said they were amazed that the teachers would gang up on him like that. Some of Jamaal's friends asked him why he didn't stop chewing gum so he would be able to participate in school activities and stop spending his time in detention.

"The rule is wrong," he replied. "I'm not hurting anybody. In fact, chewing gum helps me concentrate. I haven't been in trouble for anything else all year."

Jamaal continued chewing gum in class on a daily basis. Teachers looked for it, and he often was caught. As a result, he spent most afternoons in detention. He did not attend school-sponsored social events and missed the eighth-grade trip to an area amusement park.

On the last day of school, graduation day for eighth-graders, five of Jamaal's teachers gave him packages of gum, along with notes congratulating him on completing eighth grade.

The next year, Jamaal's brother attended Brady Middle School. The first day of school he came home very excited and told Jamaal that students were now allowed to chew gum in school. Jamaal smiled.

Reflection Questions

- What are the issues in this case?
- Discuss Jamaal's perspective of the events in the case.
- Discuss his teachers' perspectives of the events in the case.
- Based on Jamaal's behavior, at which of Piaget's stages of cognitive development do you believe him to be operating? Why?
- Consider the rules and consequences set by the school. Which of Kohlberg's levels of moral development is fostered by this kind of arrangement? Why?
- At which of Kohlberg's stages of moral development do you believe Jamaal to be operating? Why?
- What do you think of the consequences Jamaal suffered for his infractions? Why?
- How do you think these consequences were likely to impact Jamaal's relationships with his teachers? Why?
- How do you think these consequences were likely to impact Jamaal's motivation in school? Why?
- What do you think of the actions of Jamaal's teachers on the last day of school? Why?
- What do you think about the change in rules? Why?
- Do you think gum chewing should be allowed in middle schools? Why or why not?

Morality or Health?

The students in Mr. Payton's high-school health class were discussing whether sex should be considered a moral issue or a health issue. The impetus for the discussion was the fact that abstinence-only sexuality education programs are eligible for federal funding in the United States.

"Hey, Terell, don't you know that sex when you're not married is wrong?" asked Jacqueline.

"Wrong? What are you talkin' about, wrong? There's nothin' wrong with sex. You just gotta protect yourself and your lady—you know, wear a rubber," responded Terell. "Don't need no diseases or babies or anything like that!"

"No, Terell, it isn't just about diseases and babies. Sex is supposed to be part of marriage. Otherwise it's morally wrong," argued Jacqueline.

"Jacqi, you just say that cuz your dad's a minister," chimed in Sylvia. "Not everybody believes the same thing. Sex is just sex. It's not evil or anything."

"Are you saying the Bible's wrong?" asked Jacqueline.

"I'm saying that not everybody believes in the Bible. Some people believe other things, and those things are OK, too. The real problem in our country is that kids like us are having babies and getting STIs," responded Sylvia.

"Yeah, and that wouldn't happen if they didn't have sex!" retorted Jacqueline.

"It wouldn't happen if they used condoms, either," said Pete.

"Not true," contributed Jake. "Condoms aren't foolproof. You can still get a girl pregnant or get a disease. Heck, you can even die! I think that if something is that dangerous, it is morally wrong."

"You can die crossing the street, Jake. Does that make it morally wrong?" asked Terell.

At that point, Mr. Payton entered the discussion. "Well, you all probably have some valid points. Let's put them on the board." He made two columns on the board, one with the heading "Moral Issue" and the other with the heading "Health Issue." He asked the students to categorize their thoughts. This is what they came up with:

Moral Issue

- Most religions forbid premarital sex.
- Harming oneself or others is wrong.
- Infidelity is wrong.
- Bringing unwanted babies into the world is wrong.

Health Issue

- Unwanted pregnancy can be prevented, but only if we know how.
- STIs are dangerous and can kill. We have a right to know how to prevent them.
- It is high-risk for mother and baby when very young women get pregnant.
- The United States has a higher adolescent pregnancy rate than other developed countries where sex ed is more comprehensive.
- If sex is considered morally wrong, pregnant teens might not seek prenatal care.

"So, what do you think, class? Is sex a moral or a health issue?" asked Mr. Payton.

"Looks like a health issue to me, Mr. P," said Terell.

"I agree," said Pete.

"I still think it's a moral issue, but maybe it's both," responded Jake.

"I don't know. I still think sex without marriage is morally wrong," said Jacqueline.

"Come on, Jacqui," said Sylvia. "Don't you think we have the right to know how to protect ourselves?"

"Well, teaching kids about condoms is like telling them to wear a helmet and then go play in traffic," responded Jacqueline.

"Jacqui, I think it might be a little more like teaching kids to look both ways before they cross the street," said Mr. Payton. "We know that at some point, kids *will* cross the street. We want them to wait until they are old enough to judge the speed of traffic, and we want them to do it safely—not impulsively. We don't want them chasing balls into the street. We want them to stop, look, listen, and think before they act. I hope you will all take precautions when you choose to become sexually active."

"Yeah, Mr. Payton," said Terell. "We need to know how to protect ourselves, and 'just say no' doesn't cut it."

Reflection Questions

- What are the issues in this case?
- Explain both the moral and the health issues involved in sexuality education.
- Considering their cognitive, emotional, and moral development, should high-school students be taught about contraceptives in school?
- Considering their cognitive, emotional, and moral development, should high-school student have ready access to contraceptives? If so, what kinds, where, and how? If not, why not?
- What do you think of the way Mr. Payton handled this discussion? What, if anything, would you do differently?

Parental Involvement

At the beginning of the school year, Ms. Suttie invited her students' parents to a class open house so that they could get to know one another. At this open house, Ms. Suttie explained the first-grade curriculum to parents and solicited volunteers to chaperone field trips, plan parties, make costumes, help with bulletin boards, and help with other activities. She also invited parents to visit the classroom any time that they would like. "I have an open-door policy," she explained. "I want you to feel welcome in our classroom any time."

As Ms. Suttie talked briefly with individual parents, others used the sign-up sheets posted on the whiteboard to indicate those things for which she could contact them for help. Ms. Claxton was thrilled with Ms. Suttie's ideas regarding parental involvement. She placed her name on each of the volunteer lists and then spoke to Ms. Suttie.

"Hi, Ms. Suttie. I'm Cindy Claxton, Kelsey's mom. I just want you to know how happy I am that you actually want parents in your classroom. Please let me know if there is anything at all that I can do to help you out this year."

"Thank you, Ms. Claxton. That's very nice of you. I'll be in touch," responded Ms. Suttie.

The very next day, Ms. Claxton accompanied Kelsey to school. She hung her coat next to Kelsey's and entered the classroom. "Good morning, Ms. Suttie," she said. "I'm here to help. Just let me know what you'd like me to do."

Ms. Suttie was taken aback. "Well, good morning, Ms. Claxton. Let's see. Um, I haven't really gotten anything together. I guess I wasn't expecting such a quick response," she chuckled.

"Well, you let me know, OK? In the meantime, I'll just sit in the back of the room and watch."

"Um, OK. Let's find you a grown-up chair."

Ms. Suttie found an adult-size chair for Ms. Claxton, who sat in the back of the class for the entire morning. While Ms. Suttie found this a bit disconcerting, she went about her normal classroom routine as if Ms. Claxton were not present. She had assumed that Ms. Claxton would leave at lunchtime, however, she didn't. Instead she accompanied Kelsey to the cafeteria and ate lunch with her. The other students didn't seem to know what to make of this. A mom at lunch? Some of the older children pointed at Ms. Claxton and chuckled.

After lunch, Ms. Suttie gave Ms. Claxton a job. "Would you mind cutting out these shapes?" she asked. "We'll be using them for a project tomorrow."

"I'd be happy to," responded Ms. Claxton. She took the paper and the templates to the table in the back of the room and happily cut out shapes until recess. During recess, Ms. Claxton accompanied the children outside. She showed several of the girls how to play four-square. Rather than just watch, however, Ms. Claxton actually played with the girls for the entire recess period.

After recess, Ms. Claxton walked up to Ms. Suttie. "I'm sorry, but I have to leave for an appointment. I'll see you tomorrow."

Ms. Suttie's mouth dropped open. "Uh, OK. See you then."

After school, Ms. Suttie met with Ms. Lopez, another first-grade teacher, to discuss an upcoming unit on insects. Ms. Suttie explained what had happened with Ms. Claxton.

"Ms. Claxton?" laughed Ms. Lopez. "Better you than me."

"What do you mean?" asked Ms. Suttie.

"I had her older daughter two years ago. The woman was in my classroom every day. The appointment she had was probably in third grade."

"Uh-oh. Now what?"

"My best advice is to keep her busy doing things that don't involve her daughter. Have her make copies, put up bulletin boards, cut shapes, put together scrapbooks. Anything that keeps her away from her daughter. She just can't seem to let her kids grow up."

Ms. Suttie took Ms. Lopez's advice. When Ms. Claxton arrived the next morning, she was handed a list of things that needed to be done, all of which were out of the classroom—making copies, decorating the hallway, and stuffing envelopes. Ms. Claxton appeared disappointed. "I was sort of hoping to work with the kids," she said.

"Oh, but that's my job. If you can do these things, then that will make my job so much easier," responded Ms. Suttie. "I really appreciate your help."

Ms. Claxton helped out with similar tasks for the remainder of the week. The next week, she did not come to class at all.

Reflection Questions

- What are the issues in this case?
- Describe the situation from Ms. Suttie's perspective.
- Describe the situation from Ms. Claxton's perspective.
- What do you think of Ms. Suttie's open-door policy? Why?
- Was it appropriate for Ms. Suttie to discuss Ms. Claxton with Ms. Lopez? Why or why not?

- What do you think of Ms. Lopez's advice? Why?
- In what ways is it appropriate for parents to be involved in their children's education?
- In what ways is it inappropriate for parents to be involved in their children's education?
- How can teachers encourage appropriate involvement while discouraging inappropriate involvement?
- How did Ms. Suttie do in this regard?

Divorce

Connie was a talkative, cheerful student in Ms. Mahoney's third-grade class. She was an average student academically and was very responsible. Connie always turned in her homework on time and appeared to give her work maximum effort. She was also a very popular girl. Because of her outgoing personality, other students gravitated toward her.

Ms. Mahoney's class started working on multiplication in early October. Ms. Mahoney decided that, to help her students master the basic multiplication facts, in addition to working with manipulatives and other conceptual tools she would have them memorize each fact group in turn. She created timed tests covering each fact group. Students were given 30 seconds to complete each test. Students could move to the next fact group when they scored 100% on the timed test covering the current fact group. Connie flew through the first three fact groups. She thought this exercise was incredibly easy—the easiest thing she had done in math since first grade.

One Monday Connie was late for school, the first time ever. "Connie, you're tardy," said Ms. Mahoney as Connie entered the classroom. "Did you stop in the office to get a pass?"

Connie looked down at the floor. "Yeah. Here it is."

"OK, take your seat. We're just getting ready for our next math test."

Connie sat down at her desk. Ms. Mahoney placed a test facedown on each student's desk. She looked at her watch and waited for the second hand to reach 12. When it did, she said "Go!"

The students flipped over their tests and began working feverishly, except for Connie. Connie flipped over her test and stared at the problems. She had just begun working when Ms. Mahoney yelled "Stop! Time's up."

"Pass your papers forward, boys and girls," she instructed.

Connie sighed as she passed her paper forward. "Guess I'll be doing that one again tomorrow," she thought.

Ms. Mahoney was surprised when she graded the tests and found that Connie had completed only two problems. On her test, in big red letters, Ms. Mahoney wrote, "2/10—What happened?" Upon seeing her score and Ms. Mahoney's comment,

Connie's eyes filled with tears. She raised her hand and asked permission to go to the bathroom. There Connie sat in one of the stalls and cried.

When she returned to class, Connie was subdued. She did not laugh and talk as she generally did in class, which was almost a refreshing change. Ms. Mahoney assumed that Connie just didn't feel well, because many of her boisterous students became quiet when they were under the weather.

Connie's lack of enthusiasm about school continued throughout the week. "Poor kid must have a cold or something," thought Ms. Mahoney. However, Connie's school performance didn't improve over the next few weeks. If anything, it got worse. Connie neglected to turn in several homework assignments. This was understandable, given that she had stopped having her assignment notebook signed as she was supposed to.

"Connie, why isn't your assignment notebook signed?" asked Ms. Mahoney.

"I forgot," responded Connie.

"Again? You forgot yesterday, too, Connie."

"I know. I'm sorry, Ms. Mahoney. I'll get it signed tonight."

"OK, Connie. You really need to do this. It helps you remember to do your homework. You've been forgetting to get that done, too."

Connie looked at her feet. "I know, Ms. Mahoney. I know. I'll do better. I promise."

Ms. Mahoney put her hand on Connie's shoulder. "I know you will," she responded.

At lunchtime, Connie sat by herself instead of with her usual group of friends. She took a couple of bites of her sandwich and threw away the rest.

"Connie, why are you throwing away your lunch?" asked Ms. Mahoney.

"I'm not hungry."

"You need to eat to keep up your energy. Food is the body's fuel," responded Ms. Mahoney.

"I know," Connie sighed.

The next day, when Connie failed to turn in the required parental permission slip to participate in a field trip, Ms. Mahoney pulled her aside.

"Connie, you haven't been yourself lately. You've been late to school, you haven't been turning in your homework, you haven't done very well on in-class assignments, and now this. What's going on, kiddo?"

"Oh, Ms. Mahoney," Connie cried. "My mom and dad are getting divorced. It's just terrible! Dad moved out and Mom's mad all the time, and my whole life is just awful!"

Ms. Mahoney put her arm around Connie and let her cry on her shoulder. When Connie's crying subsided, Ms. Mahoney looked at her and said, "I understand, Connie. We'll work it out, OK?"

Reflective Questions

- What are the issues in this case?
- What signs did Connie exhibit that showed something was wrong in her personal life?
- How do you think Ms. Mahoney did in recognizing and responding to these signs? Why?
- How might Ms. Mahoney help Connie cope with her parents' divorce?
- What are some things that teachers need to consider when students' parents are divorcing?
- What are some things that teachers need to consider later?
- What other family issues might impact a child's ability to learn?
- How can teachers help children cope with these issues?

The Target

Ms. Kramer teaches second grade at Dawson Elementary School, a K–8 school in a small town. She has been teaching there for 20 years and loves her job. She thoroughly enjoys her young students and is an outstanding teacher. In fact, she is the most frequently requested teacher in the district.

This year she has a very lively group of students. There is one exception—Carl. Carl is a very small, very quiet little boy with an unruly mop of blond hair. He seems like a nice boy, but Ms. Kramer can barely get him to say two words. Carl reads at grade level and is responsible about doing his work in class and careful with materials. However, he never volunteers to answer questions and shies away from other attention as well. He seems to be well liked by his peers, in spite of his shyness.

Carl lives with his father, stepmother, and two stepsiblings in a small, rented, unkempt home. His stepbrother, Gerald, is in the other section of second grade, taught by Ms. Martin. His stepsister, Martha, is in seventh grade. His biological mother left when Carl was 3 years old. Carl's father married Carl's stepmother 18 months later. Carl's father drives long-distance for a trucking company, so he is gone much of the time. His stepmother is a stay-at-home mom.

Gerald and Carl could not be more different. Whereas Carl is small and blond, Gerald is large for his age and has close-cropped black hair. While Carl is quiet and withdrawn, Gerald is boisterous. All the other children seem to like Carl, but Gerald has very few friends. In fact, Gerald is a bit of a bully. Martha appears to be an average 12-year-old.

During the second week of school, Ms. Kramer assigns some math homework. Ms. Martin gives the same assignment to her class. Gerald turns in his homework, but Carl does not. He tearfully tells Ms. Kramer that he "forgot it at home." Ms. Kramer asks him to turn it in the next day, and Carl readily agrees with a smile. However, the next day Carl still does not turn in his homework. When Ms. Kramer confronts him about the missing homework, Carl again begins to cry. He apologizes and tells her he will bring it the next day. This pattern continues for several days. Finally, Ms. Kramer calls home to talk to Carl's dad. However, he is on the road, so she speaks with his stepmother.

The next day, Carl comes to school and hands a dog-eared math paper to Ms. Kramer. Ms. Kramer thanks him for bringing in the paper. He smiles at her wanly.

Grades 1–4 at Dawson Elementary participate in a reading incentive program. The students read books outside of class, their parents sign a form weekly indicating what the students have read that week, and the students receive rewards. At the end of a 3-month period, if all the students in the class have met their goals, the entire class receives a party. Each week, Gerald brings in his signed reading slip; however, Carl keeps forgetting to bring in his—along with his homework. The other students begin to put pressure on him because they want that class party.

As the school year progresses, Ms. Kramer notices that Carl's clothes have become too small for him. They are also a bit ragged and don't look clean. In contrast, Gerald comes to school in new, fashionable clothes that fit correctly and are clean and pressed.

Soon after Ms. Kramer notices this, she realizes that Carl often comes to school without a lunch or money to buy lunch. When she asks him about this, he says, "I forgot it."

Several times she gives him portions of her own lunch to eat. Before long, he stops bringing lunch altogether. She contacts his stepmother again to discuss the situation.

"That kid! I don't know what I'm gonna do with him. He can't keep track of anything. His lunch is here on the counter," his stepmother responds.

Carl still does not bring his lunch to school. About a week later, Ms. Kramer notices that the other children are bringing lunch for Carl. "What a great bunch of kids," she thinks. "They certainly look out for one another."

As the weather turns colder, Ms. Kramer notices that Carl comes to school without a jacket. Gerald has a brand-new one that he wears. "Carl, you need to bring a jacket or you won't be able to go out for recess," she tells him.

"That's OK. Ms. Kramer, I just forgot it."

Ms. Kramer has an extra jacket in her closet for "emergencies." She offers the jacket to Carl, who accepts it with a smile and runs out to recess with the other children. Gerald sees Carl outside in Ms. Kramer's emergency jacket and scowls. After school that afternoon, Ms. Kramer receives a phone call from Carl's stepmother.

"Don't you give my boy jackets and stuff to wear! If he forgets his, he just needs to suffer!"

"But Mrs. Grover, I'm just trying to help him. He needs to play outside with the other children," responds Ms. Kramer.

"The heck he does. He needs to learn to take care of his stuff! And about the other kids giving him food. That has to stop, too!"

"But, Mrs. Grover, he never has a lunch. The kids are just sharing like they have been taught."

"We don't need your charity, Ms. Kramer. We take care of our own! That boy has stomach problems and needs to eat a special diet. Those kids are makin' him sick."

"I'm sorry, Mrs. Grover, I didn't realize," responds Ms. Kramer.

"Just don't do it anymore!"

About 5 minutes later, the principal comes into Ms. Kramer's classroom.

"I just got a call from Mrs. Grover," she begins.

"Yeah, me too. Something is wrong here. Something is very wrong."

"I agree. She wants him to come home for lunch every day so that your other students don't give him any unhealthy food to eat."

"If they don't give him food, he won't have anything to eat," responds Ms. Kramer. "I think we ought to call the Department of Children and Families. She's neglecting that child—actively and purposely neglecting him! Who knows, she might even be hitting him!"

"OK, let's make the call. I'll also tell her that while I can't keep her from taking him from school, he can't walk home. She will have to come sign him out and in every day. I figure that she'll do for maybe three days."

Ms. Kramer and her principal call the Department of Children and Families, which responds by opening an investigation. Social workers visit the school and interview Carl and his stepsiblings, as well as Ms. Kramer. They also visit the home and talk to Mrs. Grover. The following week, they contact Ms. Kramer and tell her that there is no evidence of abuse or neglect. Ms. Kramer is stunned. She begins carefully documenting everything that happens to Carl.

By now, it is winter and very cold. Carl still comes to school without a jacket, gloves, hat, or boots. His stepbrother arrives fully dressed for winter weather. The parents of the other children have become aware of what is happening to Carl. It is difficult to keep secrets in a small town. Soon they, too, are looking out for Carl. One parent observes Gerald's mother picking up his sister and him after school, while Carl walks home—without proper winter apparel. Appalled, she contacts Ms. Kramer, who documents the incident and contacts the Department of Children and Families again. Throughout the school year, she contacts the Department fourteen times. Each time they tell her that their hands are tied. Neglect is very hard to prove.

Finally, toward the end of the school year, Carl comes to school with a black eye. "What happened to your eye, Carl?" asks Ms. Kramer.

"I dunno," he responds.

"Come on, honey, you can tell me."

"No, I can't. It'll just get worse," he responds tearfully.

"Can I take your picture, Sweetie?"

"OK."

Ms. Kramer takes Carl's picture and contacts the Department of Children and Families again—this time with hard evidence.

Reflection Questions

- What are the issues in this case?
- What makes neglect so difficult to prove?
- Teachers are mandated reporters. At what point would you have called the Department of Children and Families? Why?
- What signs and symptoms of abuse and neglect should teachers be aware of?
- How are this neglect and abuse likely to impact Carl's future?
- What is the best thing that could happen to Carl at this point? Why?

Sit With Us—or Else

Juanita is in seventh grade at King Middle School. This is her second year at King. Last year she was fortunate to make a few new friends, girls she liked enough that they spent time together on weekends and over the summer, as well as in school. Sadly, these girls are not in many of Juanita's classes this year. In fact, her closest friend, Marissa, is in only one of her classes.

Juanita's mother encourages her to spend time with friends and to make as many friends as possible. She would very much like to see Juanita involved with the "popular" group at school. These boys and girls attend all the school dances and high school football games together. They often host parties at their houses as well. All the girls wear the same expensive, trendy brands of clothing.

Juanita's mother thinks that inclusion in this group would be good for Juanita. Juanita, on the other hand, really doesn't care about being in this group. It isn't that she dislikes the students in the group. She doesn't know them that well. Rather, she is content to spend her weekends with Marissa. Besides, she can't afford to buy the clothes that the girls in the popular group wear.

Juanita has several classes with members of the popular group. In her social studies class, she is working on a group project with three girls in this group. At first, they seem reluctant to include Juanita in the planning and execution of the project, but as time goes on they begin to see that Juanita has much to offer. As they get to know her better, they even decide that they like her. One of the girls, Paula, invites Juanita to a party on Saturday night. Juanita is unsure of whether she wants to go. "I don't have the right clothes," she thinks. "I'll look like such a geek."

However, she agrees to ask her parents if she may attend. Her mother is thrilled with the idea and even volunteers to buy Juanita a new outfit from the store where the popular girls buy their clothes. At the thought of a new outfit, Juanita brightens and decides that, if she is dressed right, she might just have fun at the party. She calls Paula to tell her that she will be happy to attend.

Juanita's mother takes her to buy a new outfit, as promised. Juanita is very pleased with her new look, as is her mother. However, the outfit costs Juanita's mother nearly a week's salary.

"Well, we can't do this all the time, Sweetie, but this is a special occasion. You look wonderful, and I am sure you will have a good time."

"Thanks, Mom. I really appreciate this," responds Juanita.

On Saturday night, Juanita finds herself excited about going to the party. She puts on her new outfit, does her hair three times, and carefully applies her makeup. Finally satisfied, she goes to the living room to show her mother.

"Juanita, you look fantastic!" exclaims her mother.

"Are you sure, Mom? I feel a little weird," responds Juanita.

"No, you look perfect. Let's go."

On the way to Paula's house, Juanita's stomach is filled with butterflies. "Why am I so nervous," she wonders. "They're just a bunch of kids. Just like me."

"My! Look at this lovely home," Juanita's mother comments as they pull into Paula's driveway. "You have a good time, Juanita. Your dad will pick you up at 10:30."

Juanita does have a good time at the party. Several of her new friends comment favorably about her new outfit. Even Steve notices. Juanita has had a crush on Steve for months but has always considered him beyond her reach. She beams with pleasure at his comments. Before Juanita's father comes to pick her up, Clarice announces that the party will be at her house next weekend. "You're coming, aren't you Juanita?"

Juanita is very pleased. When she gets home, her mother is waiting to hear all about the party. When Juanita tells her about the party at Clarice's the next weekend, her mother is positively ecstatic. "That's just wonderful, Juanita! You're on your way! We will have to figure out a way to get another new outfit."

On Monday morning, Juanita takes special care as she gets ready for school. She wants to look just right. When she arrives at school, Marissa is waiting for her as usual. Juanita starts to tell her about the party when Paula and Clarice walk up to them. "Come on, Juanita, you don't want to be late for social studies, do you?" asks Paula.

"Oh, we've got plenty of time," answers Juanita.

"Come on, let's go!" responds Clarice.

Juanita looks at Marissa and says, "I'll see you after school, OK? At the service meeting?"

Marissa looks down and responds, "Yeah, sure. Whatever."

"What's *her* problem?" asks Paula.

"I guess she just wanted to talk," responds Juanita.

Paula tosses her head and flips her long, blond hair. "Yeah, well so do we. So—what do you think of Steve? I think he likes you."

"Really? Did he say that?"

"No. It's just the way he was looking at you Saturday night. So you're going to the community service meeting after school?"

"Yeah. Last year Marissa and I volunteered at the nursing home. We sort of adopted some grandparents. It was kind of fun."

"Hmmm, maybe we should try that, too," says Paula.

After school, Juanita and Marissa meet in Mr. Rigney's classroom for the community service club meeting. As they sit chatting, Paula and Clarice walk in.

"Hi, Juanita," says Paula. "Come sit over here with us."

"I'm sort of sitting with Marissa, Paula. Why don't you guys sit here? There's plenty of space."

"No. We want to sit over here," says Clarice. "And we want you to come sit with us."

Juanita doesn't know what to do. She looks at Marissa, who has found sudden interest in her desktop. Then she looks at Paula and Clarice.

"Come on Juanita," says Paula. "Do you want to sit with us or not?"

Juanita thinks about the party last Saturday and the one coming up this Saturday. She thinks about Steve. Finally, she thinks about how happy her mother was when she found out Clarice had invited her to the party this Saturday. She looks back at Marissa. Then she stands and says, "I'm sorry, Marissa, but I have to."

Juanita goes to sit with Paula and Clarice, leaving Marissa sitting alone and staring at the desktop, looking as if she is going to cry.

Reflection Questions

- What are the issues in this case?
- Explain the situation from Juanita's perspective.
- Explain the situation from Marissa's perspective.
- What aspects of development contribute to their perspectives?
- In what ways does Juanita conform to the expectations of her new friends? Why?
- Why might Juanita's mother care so much about Juanita's being part of the popular group?
- How is this likely to impact Juanita's friendships? Why?
- How might Juanita have handled the situation differently?

Rejection

Madison Middle School is a large school located in a medium-size city. It is a diverse school, both ethnically and economically. Because of its large student population, Madison is divided into eight teams. While the teams function fairly independently of one another, the students all share the same curriculum, extracurricular activities, band, and chorus. This allows the students to spend the bulk of their day with members of their own team but to have contact with other students as well.

David is a 13-year-old seventh-grader at Madison. Like many boys his age, David is going through a growth spurt. His rapid growth has caused him to outgrow many of his clothes. His pants are often a little too short, as are his shirts. While David's parents are middle-income, they can't afford to buy him new pants every month, as it seems he could use right now. David might also be considered fashion-challenged. Even when he has money to buy new clothes, his choices never seem to be what the other kids consider stylish. He ends up buying things that younger kids are more likely to wear, which often makes him the butt of jokes.

"Hey, Davey, where's the flood?" asked Pete, in reference to how short David's pants were.

"Davey boy, love the new backpack. I had one just like it when I was in third grade!"

David nearly always tells one of his teachers when his classmates make unkind comments to him. The teachers generally reprimand those who have made the comments, but it is unusual for them to do more unless a physical altercation is involved. Unfortunately, this happens frequently in the hall, where teachers are less likely to observe it. A favorite technique for "messing with Davey" is to come up behind him and reach around to knock his books to the ground. This happens at least twice a day and often results in David crying.

"Why do you always do that?" David cried after one such encounter.

"Cuz it makes you cry, Davey boy," came the response, accompanied by laughter.

"I'm telling!" retorted David.

"Yeah, Dave, you always do. Did anybody else see me do anything to David?"

"I didn't see anything."

"Me neither."

Upon entering the classroom, David went to speak with Ms. Johnson. "Ms. Johnson, Carl smacked my books out of my hands again."

"OK, David. I'll take care of it."

Ms. Johnson gave Carl a 15-minute lunch detention. Carl accepted his punishment with a smile and a wink at David.

David is a "B-C student" who is very compliant with rules and teacher requests. He enjoys English class, band, and chorus. David does well in English, particularly creative writing. He does not enjoy math, science, or PE—especially not PE. Because David is not very athletic, he often struggles in PE. None of the other boys want to have him on their team. When rosters are read for various games, there generally is a collective groan from the team to which David has been assigned.

"That's it. We lose," said Jared after having David assigned to his team.

"That's enough, Jared," responded Mr. Long, the PE teacher. "Everybody plays. Nobody whines."

"Yeah, yeah, yeah. First person to give Davey boy the ball deals with me," said Jared to his teammates as soon as Mr. Long was out of earshot.

Nobody passed David the ball during the game in spite of his yelling "I'm open!" repeatedly.

Reflection Questions

- What are the issues in this case?
- Explain the situation from David's perspective.
- Explain the situation from the perspective of David's peers.
- Why did David's peers reject him?
- What, if anything, could David's parents do to help him?
- What, if anything, could David's teachers do to help him?

The Boy

It is the first day of middle school for Suzanne, and in each class she hopes to see at least one friend from elementary school. However, none of Suzanne's friends from elementary school are in any of her classes. She feels terribly alone as she makes her way through the day in her huge, new school. She sits by herself at lunch because she doesn't know anyone who shares her lunch period. It isn't as if the other kids have been mean to her. It's just that most of them seem to know students in their classes.

"I hate middle school," thinks Suzanne, as she makes her way through the crowded halls from the cafeteria to science class. She remembers to stop at her locker and still gets to class on time—no easy feat in this place. She takes a seat at one of the two-person tables in the front of the class and glumly waits for class to begin. Just then a boy hustles into class out of breath and sits next to her at the table.

"Hi," he says and smiles. "I'm Steve."

"I'm Suzanne," she replies with a smile. Suddenly the world doesn't seem so terrible after all. "Steve is really, really cute," she thinks. He has longish blond hair, big blue eyes, and the cutest freckles on his face. And he seems so nice. He is the first person to talk to her all day.

Suzanne barely hears what the teacher is saying about classroom rules and procedures. All she can think about is the gorgeous boy sitting next to her. She leaves class on cloud nine and forgoes stopping at her locker in favor of visiting the bathroom on her way to math class.

When she gets to math class late because she forgot which end of the school has the up staircase and which the down, she is surprised to find that Steve is in this class as well. She takes a seat next to him. She is very happy she took the time to brush her hair rather than going to her locker. "Hi, again," she says.

"Hey, you're in here too? Cool," he responds.

Suzanne can barely contain her excitement. "He must like me too!" she thinks. She is even more excited to find that he is in her study hall.

That evening when her parents ask about her day, all Suzanne can talk about is Steve. She says nothing about not having any classes with her friends. She doesn't mention the up and down staircases or how confusing the layout of the school is. She just talks excitedly about Steve.

"It sounds as if you've got quite a crush on him, Suze," says her mother.

"Well, he is really cute and nice and, well, you know," responds Suzanne.

Suzanne's mother laughs. "Yes, honey, I know all about it. Just don't get your heart broken. Puppy love can be brutal."

"Mom! It's not like that. I just like him is all."

Suzanne's favorite classes become those in which Steve is also a student, although math and science have never been her favorites. She dreads the classes she doesn't have with him even though she has made friends with a couple of other girls. One of these girls went to elementary school with Steve. Suzanne asks her all about what he was like growing up. She also discovers that Steve lives only a block away from her grandmother. Soon she starts riding her bicycle to her grandmother's house on Saturdays in hopes of seeing him. Several times she sees him playing basketball in the driveway or raking leaves. He always smiles and waves and occasionally even asks if she would like to join him. Suzanne is in heaven.

As the first semester progresses, Suzanne and Steve become lab partners in science. They often work on their math homework together in study hall. Suzanne can hardly believe her good fortune. However, she often overhears other girls talking about how cute Steve is. Soon it becomes apparent that the bulk of the sixth-grade girls feel the same way about Steve as Suzanne does. She becomes concerned. Still, with whom does he sit in science class? With whom does he do his math homework? And who plays basketball and paper football with him? None of the other girls—just Suzanne.

The local high school has a special seating section for middle-school students during basketball games. This section is chaperoned by middle-school teachers, allowing the kids to sit with their friends yet be under the watchful eyes of adults. Parents and students find it a welcome opportunity for monitored independence. Because the majority of the middle-school students are not allowed to date, this is where they go to meet their boyfriends and girlfriends and to find out if their love interest "likes them likes them." Girls clamor to sit by Steve. Thus far, he hasn't declared anyone to be his girlfriend, but just about every girl in the sixth grade would be more than willing to fulfill the role. The rumor mill has been churning for the past few days that Steve finally will choose a girlfriend at tonight's game.

Suzanne is very nervous. She primps with extra attention tonight. She dresses in school colors, does her hair four times before she is satisfied, and tries to apply just the right amount of makeup. She doesn't want to look like a clown or a floozy, but she also doesn't want to look like a baby who doesn't wear makeup.

She and her best friend, Barb, arrive at the game together. When they enter the middle-school section, Steve is not yet there. Suzanne knows he plans on coming tonight; they talked about it in study hall. She can't wait for his arrival. "Tonight is the night," she thinks. "He is finally going to tell me he really likes me."

Steve arrives before halftime of the sophomore game and greets Suzanne with a smile and a wave. She waves and smiles expectantly. However, he doesn't sit next to her.

He joins a group of other boys, and they begin laughing and talking loudly. Suzanne is disappointed but figures he might be just as nervous about this as she is.

Between games, Suzanne and her friend go to the concession stand to get something to drink. They talk about Steve and the likelihood that he will tell Suzanne he likes her tonight. Suzanne is so nervous her stomach is doing back flips. Barb tries to calm her down. "Geez, Suze, take it easy. He's just a guy."

"Just a guy?! Are you crazy? He is *the* guy."

"Yeah, right. He's not so different from the rest of them," responds Barb.

"Yes he is! *Everybody* likes Steve. But nobody loves him like I do."

They walk back toward their section. As they enter the gym, Suzanne looks for Steve. She spots him sitting in a different place than before. She starts to smile and then freezes. He is sitting with his arm around another girl! Crushed, Suzanne turns on her heels and leaves the gym, crying. Barb trails behind her.

Steve follows, yelling "Suzanne, wait! What's wrong?"

"What's wrong? I'll tell you what's wrong—you're sitting up there with your arm around Mary Ann, that's what's wrong! I thought you liked me."

"I do like you, Suzanne, we're friends."

"I don't want to be your friend, Steve," Suzanne says and stomps off crying. As Barb follows her out of the school, she says, "I can't ever go back to school. How can I ever face him again?"

When she gets home, her mother asks who won the game.

"We won, but I lost," Suzanne replies. She walks up to bed and cries herself to sleep.

Reflection Questions

- What are the issues in this case?
- Describe the situation from Steve's perspective.
- Describe the situation from Suzanne's perspective.
- It is not unusual for the majority of girls in a sixth-grade class to like the same boy. Why might this be so?
- What traits are sixth-grade girls likely to find attractive in a boy? Why?
- What could help Suzanne deal with her feelings of loss?

What Did I Do?

M ark was a sixth-grade student at Fillmore Middle School. For weeks the student council had been preparing for the annual Valentine's Day dance. Most of Mark's friends had already asked someone to go to the dance with them. Mark wanted to go to the dance but was nervous about asking the girl he most wanted to go with—Jeanice. Mark had liked Jeanice for quite some time, but they were not "going together" like so many of their friends. In fact, they rarely talked to each other outside of class. Mark was not at all shy in most circumstances, but, for some reason, when Jeanice was around he became tongue-tied.

Mark talked to his best friend, Jared, about the situation. Jared was going to the dance with his present girlfriend, Marie. Jared had already gone through several girlfriends this school year and had lots of confidence around girls.

"Just ask her, Mark. What do you have to lose?"

"What if she says no?" asked Mark.

"Then ask somebody else. It's not a big deal!" replied Jared.

"Yes, it is. I've never asked a girl out before. I'm really nervous."

'Look, she's always looking at you. She likes you. Just ask. Today."

"I'll think about it."

Mark worried about asking Jeanice all day. He practiced what he was going to say in his head all during study hall. Finally, when the bell rang to end the school day, he decided he would do it. He found Jeanice at her locker.

"Uh, hi, Jeanice," he said shyly.

"Hi, Mark."

"Um, uh, what are you doing?"

"Just getting my stuff to go home. Why?"

"Well, I was sort of wondering, um, are you going to the dance with anyone?"

"No."

"Well, um, do you think maybe you'd like to, um, go with me?" he stammered.

Jeanice broke out into a huge smile. "Yes! I mean, sure, I'd love to, Mark."

Mark was thrilled. "Great! Well, I'll see you tomorrow."

As Mark walked home, he was very excited. His first date. His first dance. And it was with Jeanice, a girl he really liked.

When Mark's mother got home from work, Mark told her about the dance.

"That's great, Mark. What do the guys wear to dances at your school?"

"I, um, hadn't thought about that."

"Well, check it out and let me know if you need anything. Are you supposed to pick up Jeanice or are you meeting there?" asked Mark's mom.

"Um, I, uh, hadn't thought about that either."

Mark's mom chuckled. "Well, just let me know what's going on, OK?

Jared called Mark that evening. "So you're going with Jeanice, huh?"

"How'd you know?" asked Mark.

"Everybody knows. I think Jeanice has called everybody she knows to tell them. She says you're 'going together.'"

"She said that?"

"Yeah. So what are you getting her for Valentine's Day?"

"Huh? What do you mean?"

"Geez, sometimes you are so dumb! She's your girlfriend now. You have to get her something for Valentine's Day, idiot."

"Oh man! What have I gotten myself into? I don't know what to get a girl! I don't have any money!"

"Ask your mom. She's cool. She'll help you out," offered Jared.

Mark sought out his mother, who was reading. "Mom?"

"Yeah?"

"Jared says I have to get Jeanice something for Valentine's Day cuz now she's my girlfriend."

"Well, Mark, you don't have to, but it would be a nice thing to do."

"Like what? I don't know what she likes! I don't have any money!"

"Well, I can help you out there. Traditional Valentine's gifts are things like flowers or candy and a nice card. Stay away from jewelry. You're too young for that."

"Candy, like a candy bar?"

"No, Mark, candy like one of those heart-shaped boxes filled with chocolates."

"How much do they cost?"

"Don't worry. I'll help you out."

"Thanks, Mom."

Mark and Jeanice agreed to meet at the dance on Friday night. On Friday morning, Mark gave Jeanice a big heart-shaped box of candy before school. Jeanice was thrilled. She showed it to all her girlfriends. Mark was pleased that Jeanice liked his gift so much. He was looking forward to the dance.

Mark arrived at the dance early so he would be certain to be there when Jeanice arrived. When her father's car pulled into the lot, his stomach started doing flips. He was really nervous. She got out of the car and his mouth dropped open. She looked fabulous! He thought she was the prettiest girl there.

They went inside to the nicely decorated gym. The DJ was playing a slow song. Several couples were on the floor swaying to the music. Mark worked up the courage to ask Jeanice to dance. They took to the floor and mimicked what the others were doing. It felt really good. The next song was more up-tempo. Mark didn't really know how to dance, but he tried. Jeanice was a much better dancer. After two songs, they took a break and sat down.

"Would you like some punch?" asked Mark.

"Sure. Thanks."

Mark went over to the punch bowl. There he ran into Jared and a couple of the other guys. They started talking about the upcoming NCAA basketball tournament. Then Mark suddenly realized that he had left Jeanice waiting for punch. He turned around to look for her. She was sitting by herself at a table, looking glum. He quickly got the punch and returned to the table with it.

"What took you so long?" asked Jeanice.

"Oh, sorry. I was just talkin' to Jared and some other guys."

"Oh. I see."

Jeanice was pretty quiet after that. Mark tried to get her talking. He cracked some jokes. He asked her to dance again. She danced, but not with much enthusiasm. After a fast dance, Jeanice excused herself to go to the bathroom. Mark talked to Jared while he waited for her.

"Man, what's takin' her so long?" Mark asked.

"She's a girl. They spend all day in the bathroom," replied Jared, who had two sisters.

Mark waited some more. Finally, after 10 minutes, he became concerned. He asked Jared's date to look for her in the bathroom. She wasn't there. Mark became more concerned. He started looking for her elsewhere. He finally saw her as she was getting into her dad's car in front of the school. "Jeanice! Wait!" he yelled.

She got into her father's car without looking back. Mark was stunned. He looked at Jared. "What did I do?" he asked.

Reflection Questions

- What are the issues in this case?
- Describe the situation from Mark's perspective.
- Describe the situation from Jeanice's perspective.
- What are some possible reasons for Jeanice's early departure?
- What should young adolescents know about dating etiquette?
- Are school-sponsored dances a good way for young adolescents to learn about dating? Why or why not?
- If middle schools host dances, should they also teach about dating etiquette? Why or why not?
- What is the role of a teacher-chaperone at a middle-school dance?

Because He Loves Me

Carrie was happy to have a boyfriend finally. All her high school friends had been dating for years, while she stayed home or babysat on most Saturday nights. It wasn't that her friends didn't try to include her. It was that she felt like a fifth wheel going out with them when they were all couples, even though they insisted that they wanted her to join them. All that changed when she bet Brandon, though. He was the first boy who seemed really interested in her. The first time Brandon asked Carrie out, she was happily stunned. She could hardly believe her good fortune. That was two months ago, and they had been virtually inseparable ever since.

Carrie's friends were happy for her when she started dating Brandon. While he wasn't the guy they would have chosen for her, he seemed to genuinely like her and treated her well. He gave her flowers, wrote love letters to her, and basically treated her like a princess. However, he didn't enjoy group dates, so Carrie began spending more of her time with Brandon and less of her time with her other friends.

"Carrie, are you coming with us to the beach on Saturday?" asked Sheila.

"I'll check with Brandon, but I think we're doing something else," responded Carrie.

"Carrie, you never do anything with us anymore," complained Sheila.

"Well, I have a boyfriend now. Give me a break. I'm not going to be as available as I was."

"Carrie, you're never available. You spend all your time with him. We miss you. Bring him with you."

"I don't think so. Brandon doesn't like group things."

Sheila shook her head. She didn't like that Carrie spent all her time with Brandon. Sheila and Steve had been dating for quite a while and still had time for their friends. She didn't understand what was going on with Carrie and Brandon, but she didn't like it one bit.

Brandon walked toward Sheila and Carrie. Carrie broke into a smile. Brandon frowned at first, then smiled. "Hello, ladies," he said.

"Hi, Brandon," answered Sheila. "Would you and Carrie like to go to the beach with a bunch of us on Saturday?" Sheila had decided to go directly to the source.

"Oh, no. Can't do it. We have big plans for Saturday," responded Brandon with a smile.

Carrie looked at Brandon with delight. "What are we doing?"

"Can't tell you. It's a surprise."

Carrie beamed. "Isn't he just the most romantic guy?" she asked Sheila.

"Yeah," responded Sheila without enthusiasm as she walked away.

As soon as Sheila left, Brandon's tone changed. His face clouded over, and he looked angry.

"What are you doing hanging around with her?" he asked Carrie.

"She's my best friend, Brandon."

"Really? I thought I was your best friend," he replied.

"You know what I mean—besides you," responded Carrie.

"Well, I don't like her. She has a bad reputation and I wouldn't want anybody to think bad things about my girl."

Carrie looked puzzled. Brandon then smiled and kissed her. Carrie sighed and thought, "So what if he doesn't like Sheila. He loves me, and that's what's important."

In English class, Carrie was assigned to work on a project with James. They were engrossed in their project and having a good time when Brandon walked by their classroom on his way to the bathroom. As he looked into the classroom and saw Carrie and James working together, he frowned.

Later, during lunch, Brandon asked Carrie about James. "I noticed you and James having quite a good time today during fourth period," he said in an accusing tone.

"Yeah, he's a nice guy. We're working on a project together," replied Carrie.

"So that's what you call it, huh?"

"That's what it is, Brandon. We're working together on a project."

"I see. And is that why you didn't answer the phone when I called last night? Were you with James?"

"No, Brandon. I told you when I called you back. I was in the shower."

"In the shower for an hour?"

"I'm sorry it took me so long to call you back. I had to do a little homework, too."

"Is that more important than I am?" asked Brandon.

"Of course not," responded Carrie. "You're the most important thing in the world to me."

"Good. Glad we clarified that." Brandon gave Carrie's arm a pinch.

"Ow! That hurt!" said Carrie.

"Just playing, honey. I'm sorry."

Sheila overheard this conversation. Later she approached Carrie to talk about it. "I don't like what's going on with you and Brandon," she opened. "Why does he have to know what you're doing every minute? Why is he jealous of James, of all people?"

"Oh, Sheila, it's just because he loves me."

"That doesn't sound like love to me—he pinched you, Carrie," replied Sheila.

"You're just jealous because nobody has ever loved you that much!" retorted Carrie.

Reflection Questions

- What are the issues in this case?
- Explain the situation from Carrie's perspective.
- Explain the situation from Sheila's perspective.
- What do you think is happening in Carrie and Brandon's relationship? Why?
- What makes Carrie especially vulnerable to a guy like Brandon?
- What developmental factors contribute to the situation?
- If you observed the exchange between Carrie and Brandon in the cafeteria, what, if anything, would you do?
- What should adolescents know about healthy relationships?

C   A   S   E   **36**

Locker Room Bravado

Justin, a junior at Braxton High School, recently turned 17. He has been dating Cher, who is 16, for the past 6 months. Both he and Cher are virgins. Justin is absolutely certain that he is the only 17-year-old virgin at Braxton. All the other guys seem to have had much more sexual experience than he has. It isn't that Justin is disinterested in sex. He simply doesn't want to pressure Cher, whom he really likes. He isn't sure, but he might even love her.

Cher has made it abundantly clear from the start of their relationship that she is not ready for a sexual relationship. While she is willing to spend hours on the couch in Justin's embrace, kissing him, she will not allow him to go any further than fondling her breasts. If Justin tries to go further sexually, Cher simply tells him to stop. Justin always complies with her direction. He also continues to try—just in case she changes her mind.

Lately, Justin has taken a lot of teasing from his friends about his lack of sexual progress with Cher, whom they refer to as "the Virgin Cher." He tries to laugh it off, but it is getting more difficult.

One Monday after PE, Shane says, "How was your weekend with the Virgin Cher, Justin?"

"Knock it off, Shane."

"Why? She is one. And so are you!" laughs Shane.

Matt joins in the laughter. "Man, are you ever even gonna get past first base, dude?"

"Shut up, Matt! You guys are total jerks! I actually *care* about Cher. She isn't some bimbo like the girls you two go out with!"

"Ouch, that hurts deeply, Justin," laughs Shane.

Justin slams his locker shut and stalks out of the locker room. "Damn! Why does Cher have to be such a prude? It's not like we just met!" he thinks as he walks down the hall.

Later, when he sees Cher, he is inexplicably surly with her. "What's wrong, Justin?" she asks.

"I don't know, babe. It's just that I love you so much and you won't even let me touch you," he responds.

"You *love* me? Really?" she asks breathlessly.

"Well, yeah. Of course I do, Cher. I mean, we've been together for months now. Did you think I didn't?"

"Well, you never said so before."

"Yeah, well I do."

Cher smiles and snuggles up to Justin. Justin begins thinking that maybe this weekend his luck will change.

The next day in the locker room, when Shane and Matt start teasing him again, Justin responds with "Yeah, well, all that's gonna change this weekend, boys. Cher and I are finally gonna do it!"

"Yeah, right, Romeo. Not a chance!"

Justin carefully plans a romantic encounter for Friday night. He has the house to himself because his parents are taking his brother back to college. He buys scented candles, which he arranges around the living room. He rents a romantic movie. When Cher arrives, she giggles, "Justin, if I didn't know any better, I'd swear you were up to something."

"Maybe I am," he responds.

They snuggle on the sofa, watching the movie and kissing. Justin can hardly stand it. "Please, Cher," he pleads.

"Justin, I've told you and told you. I can't. I just can't."

When Justin persists, Cher stomps off in a huff, leaving a very frustrated Jeremy alone.

On Monday at school, Shane and Matt start in again. "Get anywhere this weekend, stud?" they ask laughingly.

"Yeah, actually, I did," responds Justin.

"No way!" shouts Matt.

"Way!" says Justin.

"Yeah? How far?" asks Shane.

"None of your damned business," responds Justin.

"Yeah, I bet you and the Virgin just hung out eating popcorn and watching a movie," speculates Matt.

"Guess you'll never know, jerk," says Justin.

"Come on, we're your best friends. Tell us!" demands Shane.

"Well, since you put it like that, let's just say you'd better change Cher's nickname," laughs Justin with a wink.

"No possible way!" says Shane. "Not even a chance!"

"Think what you want. I think I'd better go to the drugstore and buy some more 'supplies,'" says Justin.

By that afternoon, six different guys have come up to him and commented about his weekend experience. Justin puffs up with pride. When the seventh person comments to him, Cher is walking around the corner. Justin blanches as he sees her.

"What was that all about?" she asks.

"Oh, nothin'. They're just jokin' around," he responds.

Suddenly, it dawns on Cher what the boys have been talking about. Her face crumples in shock and anger. "How could you, Justin? I can't believe you'd do this to me! I never want to see you again!"

"What are you talking about? I didn't do anything! All I did was tell them they shouldn't call you the Virgin Cher!"

Reflection Questions

- What are the issues in this case?
- Discuss the situation from Justin's perspective.
- Discuss the situation from Cher's perspective.
- Why did Justin imply that he was no longer a virgin? Tie your answer to what you know about sexual scripts.
- Why do you think Shane and Matt teased Justin about being a virgin?
- What aspects of development contributed to each boy's behavior? How?

I Said No!

Tiffany was a 14-year-old freshman at Creighton High. She was a cheerleader for the freshman basketball team, something she enjoyed very much. Being a cheerleader at Creighton was a sure pathway to popularity, and Tiffany was no exception. She was a popular girl. In addition to being a cheerleader, Tiffany was a good student and was involved in community service. She was also outgoing, funny, and a bit of a flirt.

Tiffany had been invited to a weekend party at the house of the captain of the varsity basketball team. This was quite an honor for a freshman, and she was very excited! She knew that there would be very few freshmen in attendance. Most of the attendees would be seniors. Tiffany was determined to fit in at the party. She had promised her best friend, Michelle, that she would tell her all about the party the next day.

On Saturday, when Michelle showed up at Tiffany's house to hear about the party, Tiffany didn't sound as excited as she had been the day before.

"How was the party, Tif?" asked Michelle.

"OK, I guess."

"What do you mean, OK? I want to hear all about it. Who was there? Who did you talk to? Any cute guys?" Michelle was nearly bubbling over with excitement for her friend.

"Yeah, there were lots of cute seniors," responded Tiffany without enthusiasm.

"Did you talk to any of them?"

"Well, sure."

"Anybody in particular?"

"You know Josh Kingsley?" Tiffany asked.

"Are you kidding me? Of course I know him! He's a football player, right?"

"Yeah, that's him. I spent most of the night with him."

"Oh my gosh! Really? What's he like? He is so cute!"

"I thought he was nice at first, but I was wrong. He's a total jerk!" Tiffany started to cry.

"Tiffany, what's wrong? Why are you crying? What happened?" asked Michelle.

"Never mind. I don't want to talk about it."

"Come on, Tif. I'm your best friend. Maybe I can help."

"Nobody can help, Chelle. Nobody."

"You're scaring me. Tell me what's going on," insisted Michelle.

"Well, you know, there was beer there, right?"

"Of course, it was a senior party. They all drink."

"Well, I didn't want to look like a total geek-baby, so I had some too," said Tiffany.

"You did? You didn't puke or anything, did you?"

"No, but I wish I had! After I had a couple beers, Josh and I started kissing."

"Kissing?! With Josh Kingsley? Wow!" exclaimed Michelle.

"Yeah, well after a while, he asked me if I wanted to go upstairs. I didn't know what to do, so I said sure, and the next thing I knew we were on somebody's bed making out. That was OK, but then he started doing other stuff—you know, like putting his hand in my shirt and stuff. I told him to stop, Chelle, I did. But he didn't. He looked at me and called me a freshman baby. I started crying. He told me to hush and then just held me for a few minutes. When I stopped crying, he told me that was better and started kissing me again. I kissed him back, and then he started pawing me again. I said stop. He just laughed. Then I just lay still and he did it!"

"Did what, Tif?"

"You know—IT!"

"You mean he had sex with you?"

"Yeah." Tiffany was crying again.

"Tiffany, did you want to?" asked Michelle.

"Of course not! But I didn't know what to do. We were all alone in that room, and I went up there with him. He said I had to know what we were gonna do, but honestly, Chelle, I didn't! I thought we were just gonna talk someplace more private and maybe kiss a little. I didn't think we were gonna have sex!"

"Tiffany, you have to talk to somebody—maybe Ms. Carter, maybe a cop, but you have to talk to somebody."

"I don't want anybody to know, Michelle. Please! Promise me you won't say anything!"

"But what if you got pregnant?"

"No, he wore a condom. I'm not pregnant—thank God!"

Just then the doorbell rang. Tiffany answered the door, sniffling back tears. It was a delivery person from a local florist. He handed her a big bouquet of flowers. Tiffany closed the door and read the card: "Thanks for a great time. I'll call you. Josh."

"Of all the nerve!" yelled Tiffany. "Look at this! I can't believe he sent me flowers after what happened!"

Michelle looked confused.

On Monday, Tiffany followed Michelle's advice and talked to her advisor, Ms. Carter. She told her everything that had happened.

Reflection Questions

- What are the issues in this case?
- Describe the situation from Tiffany's perspective.
- Describe the situation from Josh's perspective.
- What role do you think alcohol played in the situation? Why?
- Based on the information you have, was this a case of rape?
- How do you think Ms. Carter should handle this situation? Why?
- What do adolescent girls need to know to protect themselves against acquaintance rape?

She Wanted To

Josh was a senior at Creighton High. He played football and also participated in track. Participation in sports at Creighton was a sure path to popularity, and Josh was no exception. He was a very popular boy with a bright future. He had been offered a football scholarship at a Division I university and was excited about the prospect.

Josh was a regular at the parties for which Creighton seniors were famous. These parties took place at least one Friday night per month—always at the home of a senior whose parents had gone away for the weekend. Most of the kids who attended the parties were seniors, but sometimes underclassmen were graced with an invitation—especially attractive younger girls. Beer was always present at these parties. The senior parties had been a tradition for several years, and older siblings usually were happy to oblige by providing the beer.

On Monday, following one of the parties, Josh and his friend Chris got together to play basketball before school.

"Hey, Josh, how was Friday night's party?"

"It was good. No, it was very good," Josh replied with a smile.

"Sorry I missed it. What was so good about it?" asked Chris.

"Well, I got lucky with one of the freshies. And I like her."

"Really? Let's hear it."

"Well, I walked into the party and there was this gorgeous girl standing there, looking all lost. I mean she was hot. So I went up to her and offered her a beer. She took it and we started talking. She was really sweet, and smart, and funny. We talked for a long time. Then we just started kissing. I asked her if she wanted to go upstairs, and she went. I was psyched!"

"She went upstairs? Awesome, dude!"

"Yeah. Well, we flopped on Jonesie's bed and started messin' around, and she gets kinda freaked and starts cryin' and stuff. So I stopped and held her and told her it was all right—that nothin' would happen that she didn't want. She calmed down and we started kissing again, and then, well, the rest is history."

"All right!"

"Yeah, so this morning when I got up, I called down to the flower shop and ordered her some flowers."

"Flowers? What for?" asked Chris.

"I told you, man. I really like this girl. I'm gonna call her tonight and see if she wants to go out Saturday," answered Josh.

When they went inside, Josh heard his name over the PA system. "Joshua Kingsley, please report to the office," said the voice.

When Josh got to the office, Ms. Carter was looking grim.

"Josh, we have a situation here. Allegations have been made."

"What kind of allegations?" responded Josh.

"Josh, Tiffany Miller says that you raped her Friday night," said Ms. Carter.

"What the heck? I did no such thing! She wanted to!" cried Josh.

Reflection Questions

- What are the issues in this case?
- Describe the situation from Tiffany's perspective.
- Describe the situation from Josh's perspective.
- Based on the information you have, is this a case of rape?
- What role do you think alcohol played in the situation? Why?
- How do you think Ms. Carter should handle this situation? Why?
- If Josh came to you for advice on how to handle the situation, what would you tell him? Why?
- What do adolescent boys need to know to protect themselves against allegations of rape?

Around the World

Ms. Owen taught third grade at Chelsea Elementary School. In an effort to make classes fun for her students, she used games frequently. One of her favorite games was Around the World. Her class usually played this as a math game, but it could easily be adapted to other subjects as well.

The way the game worked was that Ms. Owen chose a student to begin. This student stood next to the student who sat next to him or her. Ms. Owen asked the pair a math problem, such as 5×6. If the student standing answered correctly first, he or she moved on to stand by the next student, and so on. If the person sitting answered correctly first, then he or she stood, and the other person sat. The object was to make it around the entire classroom.

Ms. Owen's class played this game at least once per week—usually on Friday afternoon. At the beginning of the school year, the students were asked addition and subtraction problems. More recently they had begun using multiplication problems. Ms. Owen thought this was a great way for the students to memorize their multiplication facts.

On a recent Friday, Ms. Owen chose Ryan to start the game. Ryan stood next to Clarice, and Ms. Owen said "six times three."

"Eighteen!" yelled Ryan quickly.

"Good job, Ryan. Move on."

Ryan pumped his fist in the air. "Yeah!" he shouted. Clarice looked down at her desk. As Ms. Owen gave the next problem to Ryan and Jeremy, Clarice began drawing.

"Four times four."

"Sixteen," shouted Ryan. "Yes!"

As Ryan moved around the room, he became more and more animated. He was smiling and laughing and appeared to be having a very good time. His classmates, however, began grumbling.

"Ryan always wins at this."

"Yeah, I don't know why we even bother."

"He's just too fast. Even when I know the answer he beats me."

"Yeah, every time."

Ms. Owen seemed oblivious to the students' comments, although she did admonish them to pay attention so that they could improve their skills. Before long, Ryan had made his way around the entire class and was declared the winner.

"The winner and still champion!" he yelled.

"Ryan, that's not very nice," said Ms. Owen.

The next Friday, when Ms. Owen announced it was time to play, the class collectively groaned—except for Ryan, who yelled "All right!"

Reflection Questions

- What are the issues in this case?
- Describe the situation from Ryan's perspective.
- Describe the situation from the perspective of his classmates.
- What motivational problems are associated with this game?
- What learning problems are associated with this game?
- What could Ms. Owen do differently to make the game more motivationally and instructionally sound?

Boys' School

M r. Morrow had taught foreign language at an all boys' high school for 42 years. He loved his job. He thought that working with adolescents helped keep him young, and he credited his good health to his job. In spite of his advanced age, he was a very popular teacher. His sections of language courses generally filled before those of other teachers. This pleased him greatly.

He tried hard to make his class fun and interesting for his students. Students generally entered class knowing nothing about the language he taught. He knew that memorizing vocabulary and conjugations could be tedious. To make it less so, he devised an incentive system to keep his students interested.

Following the first quiz of the academic year, he ranked the class from highest to lowest score. Those students with the four highest scores were ranked team captains (1s). The next four highest were ranked 2s, then 3s, and so on. Teams remained together for an entire academic quarter. Team members all sat in the same column, with 5s sitting in the front of the class and each captain in the back.

Teams competed to answer questions in class. Because not all students have the same knack for learning languages, the points were differentiated. Captains earned one point for each correct answer. Other team members earned the number of points that corresponded to their number on the team; for example, 5s earned five points for a correct answer. All incorrect answers resulted in a two-point deduction for the team. Respectfully correcting Mr. Morrow earned the team five points. Mr. Morrow calculated points on an ongoing basis and added them to the quarter total. Point totals and team standings were posted on the classroom bulletin board every Monday. If students wanted to know the point totals during the week, they would simply ask, "Team totals, Mr. Morrow?" Mr. Morrow would then respond with current totals. Mr. Morrow kept track of, but did not post, individual points.

At the end of the quarter, the winning team members netted a 2 percent bonus on their final grade; the second-place team received a 1 percent bonus. For some students, this bonus resulted in a change in their letter grade. The third- and fourth-place teams received nothing. At the beginning of the next quarter, teams were reconfigured, using the final grades of the previous quarter.

Mr. Morrow sometimes had a peculiar manner of speech that his students often imitated, but generally out of his earshot. They didn't mean to be disrespectful. In fact, it was a sign of their affection for him. He realized this but still gave dirty looks to any students he caught imitating him.

Toward the end of the second quarter, the top two teams were neck and neck in points. Alex hoped his team would win, because he figured he could really use the two percentage points added to his grade. The last test had been pretty difficult. He decided to have a talk with his teammates.

"Look guys, I think it's best if John [captain] doesn't answer any more questions," he advised.

"What's up with that?" asked John.

"Well, you only get one point for a right answer, and he still takes two points off if you get it wrong," responded Alex. "We need Neil and Michael [3 and 4] to start answering. They get more points when they're right than get taken away for being wrong."

"What about me?" asked Peter.

"Sorry, Pete. You haven't been right in a long time. If you're really sure, raise your hand. Otherwise, don't do it. We need to win."

The boys all agreed to Alex's plan because they too wanted to win.

Each day, at the beginning of class, students raised their hands and asked, "Team scores, Mr. Morrow?"

Mr. Morrow obliged, and the boys on the top two teams always cheered loudly. This quarter, the winning team was not decided until the last question of the last day of classes. Mr. Morrow asked a question, and Peter raised his hand. Michael poked him in the back. "Pete, what are you doing? Put your hand down. We're only down by two." Pete kept his hand up. He was certain he knew the answer.

Mr. Morrow looked at him. "Well, I haven't seen that hand in a while," he smiled. "Go ahead, Pete."

Peter responded. His teammates realized immediately that he was correct. They began to cheer loudly. The other team groaned. They too knew that Peter was correct.

Mr. Morrow smiled broadly. Congratulations, Peter. You just won the game for your team! Let that be a lesson to you boys."

Pete left class that day happy to be the team hero and receiving congratulations from both his teammates and the other students in the class. His teammates bought him lunch that day.

Reflection Questions

- What are the issues in this case?
- To what theory of motivation does Mr. Morrow appear to subscribe?
- What goal orientation does this program foster?
- Why do Mr. Morrow's students enjoy the game so much?

- What do you think of Mr. Morrow's incentive system? Why?
- Why does Mr. Morrow differentiate the number of points for a correct response but not for an incorrect response?
- Why does Mr. Morrow not post individual points?
- How would this incentive system work in a coeducational school? Why?
- What changes might have to be made for it to work as well in a coeducational setting?
- What are the potential problems involved in using this type of incentive system?

The Only One

Jacob is a new fifth-grade student at Smith Elementary School. He recently became the foster son of a young couple in town. He likes his new home and his new foster parents. He has met a few of the neighbor kids and has begun to form some friendships.

Smith Elementary is located in a small, rural town. The town is ethnically homogeneous, as is the school. The first day of school, Jacob feels as if he sticks out like a sore thumb. All the other students and teachers in the school are European American. Jacob is African American. He is aware of other students scrutinizing him as he walks down the hall to Ms. Schmidt's class. Some of the students stare. Others make snide comments. One boy even uses an ethnic slur to refer to Jacob.

"Whoa. This is freaky," thinks Jacob. "I can't believe I'm the only one!"

As Ms. Schmidt greets her new class, she makes a special effort to welcome Jacob. After all, he is a new student—and the only African-American student in the school. She wouldn't want anybody to think she was prejudiced or anything!

"Welcome to Smith, Jacob! I hope you'll like it here. If you need anything at all, you just let me know. In the meantime, Hans, why don't you serve as Jacob's buddy and help him get used to his new school."

"Sure, Ms. Schmidt," answers Hans. "Come on, Jacob. I'll show you around the school." As the boys walk through the halls, they begin talking. "So, you're living with the O'Leary's?" asks Hans.

"Yeah. I've been there for about three weeks now. How long have you been living here?"

"Me? I was born here," replies Hans.

"You never moved?" asks Jacob.

"Nah. How about you? How many times have you moved?"

"Three times this year. I think I'll get to stay with Sean and Maureen for a while, though."

Hans invites Jacob to eat lunch with him and his friends. Jacob readily agrees. At lunch, the boys discuss football and other equally important topics. Eventually, however, the subject turns to Jacob.

"So, Jacob, what's it like bein' black?" asks Tyler.

"Huh? What do you mean, what's it like to be black?" responds Jacob.

"Well, you know . . ."

"No, I don't. It's like bein' me."

"Geez, I didn't mean anything by it. I was just wonderin' what it's like. I mean, do people call you names and stuff?"

"Not really," answers Jacob. "Course, this is the first school I've been to that doesn't have any other black kids. This is weird, man! You guys are so white you're blue. Look at that—I can see blue veins on your wrists." The boys all laugh.

As the weeks pass, Jacob seems less and less like an outsider to the other students. He develops a group of friends with whom he eats lunch and walks to and from school. He even decides to participate in the local soccer league, although he has never played soccer before. While the other kids seem to consider him "one of the guys," the adults still appear to be trying too hard not to seem racist. Ms. Schmidt doesn't discipline Jacob the way she does her other students. If the boys get too rough during a game of recess football, she makes it a point to call their names—but never Jacob's. Even the mothers seem to bend over backward to be nice to him. The other boys tease Jacob about this preferential treatment. He just smiles and tells the other boys they're jealous of his "black power over women," causing them all to laugh.

Late in the first quarter, Ms. Schmidt assigns book reports to her class. For the most part, the book reports are fairly well written. Jacob's, however, is not. In fact, Ms. Schmidt wonders if he even read the book. She immediately feels bad for thinking this. She writes a note on Jacob's paper, asking him to see her.

"You wanted to see me, Ms. Schmidt?" he asks.

"Yes, Jacob. I'm concerned about this book report."

"What do you mean?"

"Well, Jacob, there are some problems with it."

"Like what?"

"It seems as if your report might be based on the movie rather than the book, Jacob."

"Really, Ms. Schmidt? Do you think I'd do that?"

"Well, not really, Jacob. It's just that some of the things you wrote about didn't happen in the book, but they did in the movie."

"Well, maybe I just got them mixed up. I did both," responds Jacob.

"Well, I suppose that's possible, Jacob, but I need you to show me that you read the book."

"What? Are you kidding?" exclaims Jacob.

"No, I'm sorry, I'm not, Jacob."

"I get it," says Jacob. "It's because I'm black, isn't it?"

"No, no, not at all!" stammers Ms. Schmidt. "Never mind. It's OK."

Jacob turns around and walks back to his desk with a smile on his face. He looks at his friend Paul and says, "Wait till you hear this one."

Reflection Questions

- What are the issues in this case?
- What problems would a student who is the only child of his or her ethnic origin in a school be likely to face?
- How could teachers help students in this situation fit in with their peers?
- Why do you suppose the other students at Smith so readily accept Jacob?
- Why do you suppose Ms. Schmidt responded the way she did to Jacob's accusation that her mistrust was because he is black? What does Ms. Schmidt's response say about her?
- What do Jacob's final actions say about him?